MW00974271

soy desserts

ALSO BY PATRICIA GREENBERG

The Whole Soy Cookbook

soy desserts

101 FRESH, FUN & FABULOUSLY HEALTHY RECIPES

PATRICIA GREENBERG

ReganBooks
An Imprint of HarperCollins*Publishers*

SOY DESSERTS. Copyright © 2000 by Patricia Greenberg. All rights reserved. Printed in the United States of America. No part of this book may be used or reproduced in any manner whatsoever without written permission except in the case of brief quotations embodied in critical articles and reviews. For information address HarperCollins Publishers Inc., 10 East 53rd Street, New York, NY 10022.

HarperCollins books may be purchased for educational, business, or sales promotional use. For information please write: Special Markets Department, HarperCollins Publishers Inc., 10 East 53rd Street, New York, NY 10022.

FIRST EDITION

Printed on acid-free paper

Library of Congress Cataloging-in-Publication Data
Greenberg, Patricia.
    Soy desserts : 101 fresh, fun & fabulously healthy recipes / Patricia Greenberg.
        p.   cm.
    ISBN 0-06-039394-7
    1. Cookery (Soybeans)   2. Soyfoods.   3. Desserts.   I. Title.

TX803.S6 G73 2000
641.3'5655—dc21
                                                        00-040281

00   01   02   03   04   RRD   10   9   8   7   6   5   4   3   2   1

To AAG,
health, happiness, and
a long, long life together;
you're my favorite husband
in the whole world.

CONTENTS

ACKNOWLEDGMENTS

This book is filled with sweetness both literally and figuratively, and I want to thank the following people for making it possible: Andrea Nelson for her ongoing support and tireless efforts to promote my books, cooking classes, and my tofu cheesecake. Judith Regan for taking such a personal interest in the subject; I am honored to be a part of Regan-Books. Doug Corcoran, my editor, for working very closely with me every step of the way to make this book a success. Aaron Grunfeld for providing the oven. Bert Green for his close group of friends who gave me lots of mouths to feed. Margorie Ohrnstein for her recipe testing expertise; the help was invaluable. Victoria Granof for her world-class food styling, which made my desserts look gorgeous. Tom Eckerle for his excellent skills in photographing the food. Charles Woods for the design and layout of this book. Everyone at "Resch Polster Alpert & Berger LLP" and the guys at Beyond Entertainment for eating the left-overs and giving me constructive feedback. I would also like to acknowledge all my friends and colleagues in the soyfood industry who work so hard to promote our cause.

INTRODUCTION

In almost every cuisine in the world, desserts are the much-anticipated punctuation mark of a good meal. Whether it's a simple cookie and fruit or an elaborate pastry, dessert ends a meal on a high note. And these days, many people don't wait for the end of the meal to satisfy their hunger for sweets. Americans, in particular, have gotten into the habit of snacking throughout the day on an assortment of candy, cookies, sports bars, and other goodies. By now we've all heard that an overindulgence in sweets, especially those laden with fat and refined sugar, can cause or exacerbate serious health problems such as obesity, diabetes, and heart conditions.

Yes, everyone loves sweets, but what if desserts—instead of being occasions of indulgence—were actually good for you? What if—instead of simply adding inches to hips and guilt to consciences—desserts actually provided essential nutrients and even helped protect against disease? This is not merely a sweet dream, it's a reality when delectable desserts are made with soy and soy-based products.

There are many well-written and beautifully designed books on desserts, but none is devoted solely to the use of soy, and its derivatives, as the main ingredient. This book will be your faithful guide. Soy will enhance your life so much you'll wonder how you ever lived without it. Once you add it to your diet, you'll feel better, both mentally and physically: you will be consuming health-giving levels of isoflavones, while at the same time eliminating major sources of fat and cholesterol. Another important plus is that soy foods provide complete, delicious nutrition at a much lower cost than comparable foods.

Because interest in soy-based products and ingredients has skyrocketed, today these products are easy to find and buy. Soy cheeses, soy milk, and tofu, as well as ice cream, yogurt, and more, are now sold in grocery stores. Other products, such as whole roasted soybeans, soy flour, and soynut butter, can be found in any health food store. Soy foods are easy to store: some come in airtight packages that require no refrigeration, some can be frozen. And they're a cinch to bake with, performing almost identically to regular flour, milk, cheese, and yogurt. Using many of these exciting new products, you, too, can make the mouthwatering desserts found within these pages.

Soy products have also become very popular with religious and cultural groups whose diets forbid the combination of meat and dairy products, or the consumption of animal products altogether. Soy foods can be substituted in most recipes calling for dairy products, making it possible to enjoy treats that once might have been strictly off-limits. It is now possible to indulge your sweet tooth in a very healthy way, thanks to the modest soybean.

This book contains more than one hundred delicious and easy dessert recipes for you to enjoy. Based on the most loved, classic desserts, taken from a wide variety of cuisines, the recipes show you how substituting soy-based ingredients in your old favorites can be a breeze. I've been working with soy for fifteen years and I'm still amazed at what these products can do. You may be completely new to the world of soy products or you may be familiar with some forms, but not with others. You can innovate and experiment with your own recipes by following the suggested guidelines throughout the book, and the Soy Source Guide in the back will help you obtain all the different products available today. With the addition of soy products, the desserts in this book—from the luscious Tofu Chocolate Almond Mousse (page 142) to the yummy Soy Chocolate Raspberry Brownies (page 105) to the rich Four-Layer Soy Yellow Cherry Cake with Soy Chocolate Cream Cheese Frosting (page 43)— are sweets that truly combine good health with great taste. If you have read this far, you now know that adding soy protein to your diet has many remarkable benefits. At this point, however, you may be wondering what exactly *are* soy foods? What forms are best? How do I use them? To get the answers to those questions and more, read on.

A Brief History of Soy

Starting out in China, and crossing several continents over thousands of years, the soybean has come a long way from its humble beginnings. This plant, whose scientific name is *Glycine max,* is a hardy member of the legume family. The soybean plant was a wild weed in eastern China that was cultivated and domesticated around the fifteenth century B.C., when farmers discovered soybeans had a propensity to replenish the soil they grew in. This indicated a high content of protein, which led the Chinese to develop what they called *"sou"* into food. The ancient Chinese displayed their enthusiasm for this new discovery by coining the terms "Yellow Jewel," "Great Treasure," and "Great Beans." When tofu was invented, the use of soy as food spread throughout China, and it became the major source of vegetable protein for hundreds of years. In Chinese, bean curd is called *"doufu,"* and the Japanese call it *"tofu,"* which is now the commonly used term. Tofu is the most important soy food, and the most widely recognized, because it has enabled the Chinese to feed their entire population from a small portion of land for centuries.

In the first century of the Common Era, the Japanese started to take on Chinese customs, especially in the upper classes. Buddhism, with its accompanying adherence to vegetarianism, was strictly followed. Bean curd, or tofu, became a major food source for the Japanese as well. Eventually, the use of soy as a food spread throughout all of Asia. Soybeans as a component of the Western diet came much later.

Soybeans were brought to Europe during the 1700s, and then to the United States in the early 1800s. During this time period, French scientists discovered that soybeans have a low carbohydrate content, and recommended them for a diabetic diet. As a result of this discovery, more and more research was devoted to soy. When the beans were brought to the United States, they were used to brew "soy coffee" and soy sauce and, because of their high nitrogen content, to replenish crop soil. In the late 1800s, American farmers grew soybeans as a high-protein feed for livestock. Oddly enough, it was Henry Ford who saw the full potential of soy. He used soybeans for fuel and car parts, and discovered early on the nutritional value of soybeans and used them for food.

Today, the United States is one of the largest producers of soybeans in the world. Most of the soybeans grown here are processed into soy oil, used widely in vegetable oils, shortenings and margarine, and high-protein animal feed. Soy is used not only for food, but also in industrial supplies and even in ink for printing. Today the University of Illinois, at Champaign-Urbana, has an internationally renowned soyfood research laboratory and a soybean museum.

Characteristics of Soybeans

The cultivation of soybeans, unlike that of most agricultural crops, has been found to improve the soil in which they are grown. Most crops need to be rotated, or grown on different land, every few years so that the land can lie fallow and restore some of its fertility. Soybeans keep the soil rich in nutrients and can be grown over and over again without rotation. In fact, when the plant was first introduced to this country, it was called "green manure" because of its beneficial effect on the soil.

The bulk of the soy crop is harvested in late September or early October, when the leaves have fallen and the mature beans have dried on the vine. Soybeans can be differentiated by color and size. The dried beans are usually yellow-beige, although there are green, purple, brown, black, and even spotted varieties.

Green soybeans, also known as edamame, are being gobbled up by the American public because of all the promising research results on the health benefits of soy. These beans are easy to eat fresh because they are harvested in early July, when the pods are immature, and sold when they are still slightly softer. Green soybeans are similar in size and color to green peas.

Yellow soybeans are brought to full maturity, and the dried beans are sold in bulk to farmers, ranchers, and food manufacturers for a wide variety of uses. Yellow soybeans are used not only whole but to make soy milk, tofu, soy cheeses, and yogurt.

Of all legumes, soybeans have the highest concentration of protein: most beans contain 20 percent protein by volume, while soy has more than 40 percent. Soy products are cholesterol-free and high in calcium, phosphorus, and fiber. Unlike Asians, most people of American and European descent did not grow up accustomed to soy as a major part of their diet. My earlier book, *The Whole Soy Cookbook*, demonstrated that soy could become a delicious, healthy staple in any diet. This book, *Soy Desserts*, shows how we can have our cake and eat it, too. In other words, we can indulge in rich, sweet treats and rest assured that we are maintaining a healthy diet. Adding soy protein to your diet makes sense for everyone.

Health Benefits of Soy

How to explain the exploding popularity of soy? The most crucial reason is clearly health-related. Using soy in all of its available forms to create mouthwatering, stylish desserts appeals to people interested in eating healthy as well as simply delicious food. In recent years Americans have become more knowledgeable about the relationship between good health and diet. The updated Food Guide Pyramid, the government-sponsored nutritional graph that appears on many food packages, and the supermarket "5 a day" fruit and vegetable program recommend relying on a more plant-based diet for optimum nutrition. More and more Americans have taken this dietary concept to heart and have begun basing their meals on vegetable-based proteins.

Soybeans provide the best and most versatile vegetable protein around. The amino acid content is sufficient for human tissue growth and repair, and research has proven that soy protein helps reduce cholesterol. Soybeans also contain compounds called "isoflavones" that are showing substantial promise in fighting certain cancers, such as breast and prostate cancer, and alleviating symptoms of menopause.

Soy is a good source of other essential nutrients: vitamin E, lecithin, omega-3 fatty acids, and dietary fiber. Additionally, soy has a low glycemic index, which helps regulate blood sugar levels. The fact that soy has no cholesterol and is lactose-free is a godsend for anyone who suffers from a milk allergy or dairy-related digestive problems.

One of the most significant advantages soy offers is that it can be readily substituted for many grain and dairy products that are traditionally used in desserts, thus avoiding any adverse reactions.

In addition to all of its health benefits, it is easy to work with soy. In fact, almost any recipe can be adapted to use soy products. Soy can do anything dairy products can do—and more. For example, some classic Italian desserts feature sweetened ricotta or cream cheese. Well, extra-firm tofu, when crumbled and sweetened, takes on a flavor and consistency remarkably similar to the ricotta used in cheesecakes. In French recipes creamy soy milk and tofu can be used to create rich custards, and soy yogurt and sour cream can be combined with fruit and used as a cream filling.

Soy products work well in either chilled or room-temperature desserts. They can be incorporated into any dessert sauce as a thickening agent or stabilizer because of their high protein content. Tofu can be used as a healthy substitute for eggs in baked goods. Soy products are neutral in flavor and therefore absorb flavorings, such as ground cinnamon and ginger, and extracts like vanilla, almond, and citrus, beautifully. Soy desserts generally stay fresh a few days longer than dairy desserts because they don't spoil as fast. These differences make the case for using soy in nutritious and luscious desserts even more appealing.

Whether you're an experienced baker or a total newcomer to dessert making (especially health-conscious desserts), this book will dazzle you with new ways of enjoying soy. Its purpose is to make it easy—as well as delicious—to include soy in the diet.

None of the recipes in this book use any dairy products, although a few do contain eggs. For those who are vegans, the strict vegetarians who eliminate all animal products from their diets, egg replacers can be used. Be sure to check the labels of soy products because a few of them contain trace amounts of milk protein.

Lacto-vegetarians—those who eat dairy products—can benefit from this book, too. You can combine dairy products with the soy products, substituting equal amounts of each in recipes that call for soy milk and cheese. You'll still receive plenty of the healthy benefits of soy. However, please keep in mind that soy serves exactly the same functions as its dairy counterparts, providing high protein, calcium, vitamins, and great flavor, but without *any* saturated fat or cholesterol. And soy products provide those helpful isoflavones.

If you are a sometime vegetarian, you, too, will enjoy this book, since it will introduce you to a whole new range of healthy food choices. Because soy products perform so well in cooking and baking, you will miss nothing and gain plenty by including soy in your diet.

In the "Stocking the Kitchen for Baking with Soy" section, beginning on page 18, you'll find a complete guide to all the products used in this book, including information on what they are, where to buy them, and how to store them. You'll want to experiment with them to suit your individual needs. Each of my recipes includes a nutritional analysis, so that it's easy to see just how these desserts fit into your overall diet. Best of all, they're unbelievably delicious, as you'll see when you whip up some of the fabulous recipes in this book. As you delight in creamy Raspberry Marble Tofu Cheesecake (page 57), tangy Lemon Ginger Soy Ice Cream (page 149) with Lemon Soy Biscotti (page 128), or homey Soynut Pecan Pie (page 73), or Soy Chocolate Peppermint Brownies (page 107), or Apricot Soy Scones (page 109), you'll be thrilled.

These recipes incorporate soy milk, soy cream cheese, soy yogurt, and tofu, among other soy foods. The results taste for all the world as if butter, cream, and real dairy products were used—yet the desserts provide all the benefits of soy. You won't believe that dense Tofu Berry Trifle (page 136) could be so incredible—and yet provide 9.7 grams of protein and absolutely no cholesterol. There's a to-die-for treat to suit every taste.

Most of these desserts are amazingly simple to make. In contrast to traditional mousses and puddings, which require slowly cooked eggs and careful mixing to achieve the proper consistency, pureed tofu allows you to whip up luscious, creamy desserts with very little effort. Tofu takes the place of eggs in the Tofu Orange Crème Brûlée (page 139), and the Tofu Chocolate Almond Mousse (page 142) with a lot less fuss.

Soy ingredients function just as their dairy counterparts do: soy cream cheese produces rich cheesecakes almost identical to the familiar favorite, soy sour cream makes a tangy topping for the Miniature Peach Upside-down Soy Cakes (page 59), and soy yogurt and soy milk add richness and moistness to many of the baked treats. Soy chocolate chips, in which soy replaces some of the fat and all of the milk in ordinary chocolate, can be used in cookies and bars or melted just like regular chocolate chips. And it's just as hard to stop nibbling them once you open the bag. Try all these unbelievably delicious desserts. You'll satisfy your sweet tooth as well as your conscience.

There is an endless supply of other healthy ingredients that make these desserts even more wholesome. For example, on the market now there are such products as organic chocolates, many different types of whole grain flours, nonhydrogenated margarine and oils, organic nuts and coffee, unrefined sweeteners, such as light and dark granulated cane juice, that can take the place of sugar, and many others. You will learn how to obtain these healthy ingredients and how to use them. In addition, this book contains up-to-date information on how to use any specialized equipment for baking and preparing desserts, such as parchment sheets to prevent low-fat baked goods from sticking to pans, and frosting techniques for decorating cakes.

How to Get Optimum Nutrition from Soy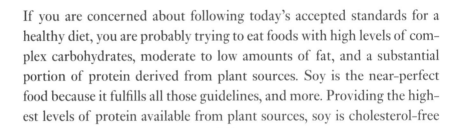

If you are concerned about following today's accepted standards for a healthy diet, you are probably trying to eat foods with high levels of complex carbohydrates, moderate to low amounts of fat, and a substantial portion of protein derived from plant sources. Soy is the near-perfect food because it fulfills all those guidelines, and more. Providing the highest levels of protein available from plant sources, soy is cholesterol-free and full of vitamins, minerals, and fiber.

You can see for yourself just how soy foods fit into a healthy lifestyle because of their versatility. Using the nutritional analysis included at the end of each recipe, you will be able to determine the calorie count, protein, carbohydrate, fat, fiber, cholesterol, and sodium for each serving. Let's look more closely at what this means, especially as it relates to soy.

CALORIES

Most soy products pack a big nutritional wallop for the number of calories they contain. In nutritional lingo, they are considered "high nutrient density" foods, in contrast to, say, a candy bar, which contains low levels of nutrients in a high calorie count. Calories are a measurement of the amount of energy a food yields. The only nutrients that provide calories are proteins, carbohydrates, and fats. (Vitamins, minerals, and water have no calories, but are essential to the body in other ways.) The heat that is released when the food is metabolized measures calories. Your metabolism, or the rate at which you metabolize food, is related to height, age, weight, and hereditary factors. You need to consume sufficient high-quality calories to give you energy for your body's needs, but not so much that your body stores the excess as fat. Soy is one of nature's most efficient foods because it provides a high level of nutrition at a relatively low caloric cost.

PROTEIN

Soy foods provide the highest levels of protein available from plant sources. Humans cannot survive without protein—it contains the essential building blocks that allow children to grow and injuries to heal. Tofu, soy milk, soy cheeses and yogurts, soy flour, soynuts, soynut butter, all products used in this book, provide protein. Soy protein is unique in that it provides isoflavones, in addition to all the nutrients needed for growth and tissue repair.

Health experts recommend that to receive the disease-preventing benefits of soy, men and women consume at least 25 grams of soy protein per day. (Proteins are measured in grams and yield 4 calories per gram.) This is easy to accomplish by reading the nutritional values on labels and recipes. Although the desserts in this book are based on soy products, I would not recommend relying on them solely for your protein needs. Desserts are an addition to a meal, not a replacement.

CARBOHYDRATES

Carbohydrates consist of both simple and complex sugars. Refined sugars, candy, and other sweets are simple sugars. All plants, fruits, grains, and vegetables—and of course soybeans—are complex carbohydrates. These days, most doctors and nutritionists advise that for a healthy diet, you should always get the majority of this group from complex carbohydrates.

All carbohydrates provide energy by breaking down into glucose (simple sugar) in the bloodstream. The pancreas is signaled and releases insulin to absorb the glucose in the body as needed. If there is a slight excess of glucose in the bloodstream, it will be stored in the muscles. If there is a tremendous excess of glucose not used readily for the body's energy needs, it is converted into fat. (In extremes, high levels of glu-

PROTEIN:
A HOT TOPIC

The basic differences between animal proteins and plant proteins are as follows: Animal protein, in the form of meat, chicken, and fish, is complete all by itself, while vegetable proteins need to be combined with other foods to create complete proteins. In other words, animal protein provides all the essential amino acids (protein building blocks) for tissue growth and repair, while most plant proteins do not. Soybeans are unique because they are high enough in amino acids to provide adequate nutrition in the absence of meat and dairy products, and they are cholesterol-free and very nutrient-dense. How do you obtain complete protein from vegetable sources? Cultures around the world, from primitive to advanced, have known the answer to that question for ages: by combining beans with grains. When consumed together, they provide all the necessary amino acids for complete protein. Soy foods make this especially easy, since they synthesize more protein than any other type of bean or legume, especially when combined with wheat or rice.

Following the recipes and serving suggestions in this book will start you on your way to incorporating more soy into your diet in a fun way. My earlier book, *The Whole Soy Cookbook,* contains recipes that are designed to ensure that you get substantial levels of soy protein in your diet. *Soy Desserts* will show you how to finish off the meal with a healthy ending. Once you understand the basic concept, you can incorporate soy a little or a lot at a time.

cose can also lead to diabetes.) Complex carbohydrates provide many nutrients as the body breaks them down, and unlike candy and sweets, are not likely to create excessive glucose in the bloodstream. Soy foods, in particular, are ideal complex carbohydrates because they contain a high level of nutrient density and enough protein to result in a lower level of sugar released into the bloodstream. Carbohydrates are measured in grams and yield 4 calories per gram.

FAT

Today's accepted nutritional guidelines suggest that you eat a diet low in saturated fats, and that you obtain most of your fats from plant sources. Fat is a necessary nutrient. It protects the lining of every cell in our body, it emulsifies food for digestion, it provides a layer of protection for the body against harsh temperatures and physical harm, and saves us in times of starvation. Fat becomes "bad" when it is consumed in larger quantities than we need. In addition, some fats are better for you than others.

Animal fats are saturated (solid at room temperature) and contain cholesterol. Saturated fats and cholesterol seem to contribute to increased risk of heart disease, cancer, high blood pressure, and strokes because they can build up in the bloodstream and cause blockage. With rare exceptions (palm oil and coconut oil, for example), fats from plants are unsaturated and cholesterol-free, and thus are a much healthier choice. Following the recipes in this book, you will automatically lower your intake of saturated fat. Fats are also higher in calories than protein and carbohydrates and can easily contribute to weight gain. Fat is measured in grams and yields 9 calories per gram.

CHOLESTEROL

As previously stated, soy foods are free of cholesterol, which in excess can contribute to heart disease. Cholesterol is found in animal products; with rare exceptions, plants do not contain it. A good nutritional guideline is not to consume more than 400 milligrams of cholesterol per day. Cholesterol is measured in milligrams, and you should always be conscious of the amount that you eat. Most of these recipes are cholesterol-free, with the exception of the few that contain eggs.

FIBER

By including whole wheat flour, soy flour, and other soy derivatives in your diet, you will automatically increase the amount of fiber that you need to maintain good health. Dietary fiber is the nondigestible part of a carbohydrate, usually derived from the bran, stems, leaves, seeds, or peels of the fruit, vegetable, or grain. Fiber is beneficial to your health because it aids in digestion of all foods. Dietary fiber cannot be broken down by humans, so as it works its way through the digestive system, it cleans out residue that is eventually eliminated. A diet high in fiber can help prevent serious diseases of the digestive tract, from diverticulosis to colon cancer. Nutritionists recommend trying to consume at least 15 grams of fiber a day.

SODIUM

Most soy foods contain relatively low amounts of sodium. The body requires only very small amounts of sodium, which it uses to keep the bloodstream functioning properly. However, it is very difficult to keep the level of sodium in your diet low because it occurs naturally in many foods and, furthermore, food manufacturers add it to almost everything. When there is too much sodium in the bloodstream, the body reacts by increasing the blood pressure to accommodate the excess. Prolonged periods of elevated blood pressure can result in cardiovascular and related diseases, such as strokes, heart attacks, and aneurysms. The sodium content in animal products is much higher than in plant-based foods, but the sodium content of processed foods is also much higher than that of fresh foods. Sodium is measured in milligrams and should not exceed 3,000 milligrams (3 grams) per day. Drinking a sufficient quantity of water daily (8 glasses) can also help reduce excess sodium in the bloodstream.

Now that you have a fuller understanding of how these nutritional terms apply to the recipes, you can make use of the nutrient analysis to help you determine how much of each nutrient you are getting in a given dessert. Every little bit of soy protein is a plus. Soy-based snacks and desserts become guilt-free indulgences because you are getting the benefits of soy.

To obtain all of those benefits, however, you need to do a little planning. Make a shopping list and begin to experiment with different forms of soy. Above all, have fun and be flexible. You don't have to make radical changes in your eating habits to reap the many benefits of soy. Whether you're a vegan, lacto-vegetarian, lacto-ovo-vegetarian, semi-vegetarian, or just interested in adding soy products to a conventional healthy diet, I guarantee that you'll be delighted by how deliciously these soy-based desserts fit into your life.

Products Made from Soy

Because more and more people are becoming aware of the benefits of soy, food manufacturers are producing new soy products rapidly. Thousands of new soy-based items have found their way into stores in the past decade. Add these newcomers to existing products made from soy, and it's easy to become overwhelmed or confused. Which ones should you add to your diet, and how? This section will highlight the products used in this book.

You are probably familiar with some of these soy products, while you may find others to be new and innovative. Either way, you'll find that it is a breeze to incorporate many of the products into everyday meal planning. You'll also see that it is neither practical nor necessary to cook with all of them all the time. You may have many questions. Can you roast soybeans like any other nut? How long does soy milk keep? Does soy cheese melt and bake like dairy cheese? How do you store tofu? In the following section, you will learn what the various types of soy foods used for desserts are, where to find them, and how to store and use them. I have referenced brand names of some products, to make it easier for you to look for them, and I have also provided a complete list of suppliers on page 157.

Let's start with the source, the whole soybean. Soybeans are available whole, green, and roasted (also known as soynuts).

SOYBEANS
Whole soybeans are obviously the simplest form of soy foods. They are a small yellow bean and are as hard as a rock. They are substantially

higher in protein than other types of beans and a great source of disease-preventing isoflavones.

Whole soybeans are available in several different forms. The most basic are canned soybeans and dried soybeans. Canned soybeans, which have already been cooked, come in 14-ounce cans. Dried soybeans are mature beans that have been harvested and dried, like other dried beans. They are sold in 1-pound plastic packages and are usually available in the health food aisles of the grocery store or supermarket.

Even when fully cooked, dried and canned soybeans remain firmer than any other bean. Once you realize that the slight chewiness of the beans does not mean that the dish is undercooked, you can appreciate the added texture. Once cooked, soybeans should be consumed within a day or two.

GREEN SOYBEANS, EDAMAME

Another form of whole soybean, these are picked before they are fully mature and usually left in their pods. They are high in protein and isoflavones. They resemble Chinese snow peas and are usually sold in bulk, like fresh produce, or frozen in 1-pound plastic bags. Look for green soybeans, fresh or frozen, at Asian markets or health food stores. While this is a dessert cookbook, these beans deserve a mention because edamame is such a popular food nowadays.

Green soybeans make a nutritious, high-protein snack. Or serve them as an appetizer before dinner, as traditional Japanese restaurants do. Prepare them by steaming for 20 minutes until slightly softened, then chill. Serve them lightly salted.

SOYBEANS, ROASTED

Also known as soynuts, these are a delicious, high-protein alternative to roasted peanuts. To make them at home, soak whole soybeans in water, drain them, and then roast them in a little oil. They are not a low-fat item, but they are high in protein (37 percent versus 26 percent for roasted peanuts) and isoflavones. Soynuts are sold in 1-pound plastic bags, in jars, or in bulk. They make delicious snacks, hors d'oeuvres, or a high-protein enrichment in many recipes. They keep at least a month.

SOYNUT BUTTER

Soynut butter is the soy version of peanut butter. It is made by roasting soynuts and then putting them in a grinder to get the nut butter consistency. There are several brands available, as well as different consistencies. Smooth, chunky, salted, unsalted, honey-sweetened, to name a few. Look for those that have no added sugar or oils.

SOY MILK

Soaking and cooking whole soybeans makes this creamy liquid. The beans are then ground and the milky liquid is pressed out. It contains no cholesterol; contrast that to low-fat dairy milk, which contains 18 milligrams of cholesterol per cup. Soy milk is high in protein and contains calcium naturally, though more calcium is often added.

Soy milk comes in whole, low-fat, or nonfat varieties, either plain or with vanilla, chocolate, or other flavorings. It is sold just like its traditional counterpart, cow's milk, in plastic jugs, paper containers, and 1-quart airtight cartons that can be stored in the pantry for up to 1 year. It is also the main ingredient in soy-based infant formulas, which are widely available in all types of markets. Look for soy milk in grocery stores, health food stores, and specialty markets.

Soy milk has a nutty flavor and can be used as a substitute for dairy milk in shakes, cream soups, sauces, and cereals. (Conversely, in recipes that call for soy milk, you can substitute regular milk if you don't have soy milk on hand, but of course you eliminate valuable soy protein by doing so.) You can choose to use regular, low-fat, or nonfat soy milk in almost any of these recipes, with a few exceptions. In cooked desserts, such as custards or flans, it is important to use regular or low-fat soy milk rather than nonfat, because it results in a firmer consistency. Once opened, soy milk should be refrigerated and consumed within a week.

SOY CHEESE

Just as dairy milk is processed into various kinds of cheeses, soy milk can be made into similar products. Although soy cheese closely resembles regular cheese in texture and uses, it is cholesterol-free and lower in fat than its dairy counterpart. There is a trace of milk protein in some soy cheeses, so those who wish to avoid all dairy products should be sure to check the labels carefully and look for the vegan varieties.

Soy cheeses are available in full-fat, low-fat, and nonfat varieties. There are firm soy cheeses that replicate mozzarella and cheddar, and come in 8- to 12-ounce packages, just like milk-based cheeses.

Soy cream cheese, remarkably similar to its dairy counterpart, is cholesterol-free and works well as a spread, either by itself or whipped up with other ingredients. It is sold in 8-ounce plastic tubs and is available in grocery stores and health food stores. Soy cream cheeses now come in a wide variety of flavors, so you can have fun with them.

You can use soy cheeses in a variety of ways. Even full-fat soy cheese contains significantly less fat than its dairy counterpart.

SOY SOUR CREAM

Adding a souring agent to soy milk (the same technique used for dairy sour cream) makes soy sour cream. It contains no lactose or cholesterol and has about 1 gram of soy protein per serving.

Soy sour cream comes in 8-ounce and 16-ounce plastic containers. It is available in the gourmet cheese or kosher section of many markets and in all health food stores. You can use soy sour cream exactly as you would dairy sour cream, since it has the same consistency and cooking properties. It is delicious as a topping for desserts or as an ingredient in baking. You can substitute equal quantities of soy sour cream in any recipe calling for dairy sour cream or yogurt. It should be stored in the refrigerator, where it will keep for 2 weeks after opening.

SOY YOGURT

Like dairy yogurt, adding live bacteria cultures to soy milk makes soy yogurt. It is lactose- and cholesterol-free. Soy yogurt comes in 6-ounce and 8-ounce cups, either plain or fruit-flavored, or in 32-ounce bulk containers, in plain or vanilla flavor. It is available in whole or low-fat varieties. You can use soy yogurt just as you would dairy yogurt. The consistency and cooking properties are the same as with dairy yogurt. Soy yogurt lasts about 2 weeks under refrigeration.

TOFU

Tofu is curdled soy milk. It is made by adding nigari (a compound from seawater), calcium sulfate, and vinegar or lemon juice to the soy milk, squeezing out the moisture, and gently pressing the remaining curds into soft blocks. Also known as bean curd, tofu provides the essential protein needed for human growth and maintenance. A 7-ounce serving of tofu provides 16 grams of protein, but it contains no cholesterol. You can buy tofu several ways:

Airtight containers—These generally come in 12.3-ounce, aseptically sealed cartons, which can be stored unopened on pantry shelves for up to 10 months. This type of tofu is available in several consistencies: soft and silken, firm, and extra firm. Many grocery stores and all health food stores carry this product.

Water-packed in plastic—One type of tofu is packed in water and sealed in your choice of 8-, 10-, 14-, 16-, 18-, and 19-ounce plastic containers. It also comes in firm, soft, and silken consistencies. The other type is tofu packed in water and wrapped in an airtight, heavy-duty plastic seal, such as Wildwood Brand. Many grocery stores and all health food stores carry water-packed tofu.

Fresh—Freshly made tofu is sold in bulk out of open containers. This type is sold only in specialty or ethnic markets.

Tofu is the basis for several frozen desserts, both homemade and commercial. All of the recipes in this book will specify which consistency of tofu—firm, soft, or silken—to use for best results. Don't worry if you don't have the exact consistency called for; they are interchangeable in a pinch. Although you will get the best results if you use the type specified, you can use what you have on hand if necessary. As a general rule, use firm tofu if you want a stiff consistency, and soft tofu for a more viscous consistency like pudding. Use silken tofu for pureed or blended dishes. Tofu must be refrigerated after it is opened, and stored in water, which should be changed every day. Once opened and refrigerated, tofu will keep about a week.

MISO

Made from fermented soybeans, miso is a salty soybean paste of Japanese origin. Miso contains 12 to 21 percent protein, comparable to chicken (20 percent), and substantial quantities of isoflavones. It is high in sodium and B vitamins.

You can buy miso in 8-ounce plastic tubs from Asian markets, grocery stores, and health food stores. With a texture like soft peanut butter, it comes in a range of colors and flavors. There are many variations in miso: strong, mild, red, yellow, or white, made only with soybeans or combined with other grains. Mixed with fruit, it makes a great base for sauces used on cakes and ice cream.

SOY FLOUR

Soy flour is made from dried, ground soybeans and is rich in high-quality protein and other nutrients. Soy flour comes in 1- to 2-pound packages, like ordinary flour, or in bulk at natural food stores. Because it is moister and denser than grain-based flours, and doesn't contain the gluten content of wheat flour, it cannot be used by itself in baked goods. It can replace up to 50 percent of the all-purpose flour called for in most recipes for cakes and muffins. It is especially easy to add to whole wheat pastry flour. It needs to be kept in the refrigerator or wrapped very tightly to keep air and moisture out.

The following soy-based foods are essential to a well-stocked pantry, but don't count on them to supply protein or isoflavones. They do have an important advantage over their nonsoy counterparts, which is that none of them contains any saturated fat or cholesterol.

EGG REPLACERS

Egg replacers are a powder made from lecithin, a soy product, and potato starch. These act to replace the emulsifying properties of eggs in baked goods. This product does not supply much isoflavone unless it is fortified. The benefit in using an egg replacer is to have a cholesterol-free vegan product.

Egg replacer powder is usually available only in health food stores, and should not be confused with liquid, egg-based egg substitutes sold in the dairy case in supermarkets. Mixed with water, egg replacers can be used in place of eggs in baked goods. The powder keeps for 6 months.

SOFT SOY MARGARINE, NONHYDROGENATED

There is only one brand that I use in baking: Spectrum Oil Brand Spread. This margarine is made primarily from canola oil with soy solids. Its advantage over other types of margarine or butter is that it contains no saturated or hydrogenated trans-fatty acids. It does not provide isoflavones; however, it is much better for you than the artificially flavored, artificially colored, hydrogenated versions of margarine.

Most commercial margarines are made primarily of soy oil and are widely available in supermarkets. If you use them, use them sparingly, as you would any fat. They generally last about 3 months under refrigeration.

SOYBEAN OIL

This oil is extracted from the soybeans (the leftover protein solids go into animal feed) and sold as pure soybean oil or as an ingredient in vegetable oil, or it is processed into margarine and shortenings. Like soy margarine, soybean oil has no saturated fat, but it does not provide soy protein or isoflavones. Soybean oil is sold in the cooking oil section of supermarkets and health food stores. Many familiar brands such as Wesson are 100 percent soybean oil.

You can use soybean oil for baking because it provides the necessary shortening properties to make baked goods moist, yet it is cholesterol-free. It should be used within 6 months or replaced.

Stocking the Kitchen for Baking with Soy

A well-stocked kitchen makes cooking with soy products even easier. Most soy products keep well in the pantry, refrigerator, or freezer. If you keep all the other necessary ingredients on hand, you'll be able to whip up most of these recipes without making a special trip to the market. The following list of pantry basics will assist you in planning ahead.

DRY STAPLES

All of these products have long shelf lives when stored in a dry, cool area. Do not buy extra-large packages; open packages may tend to attract insects, especially in summer months. After opening, it's best to keep them in airtight canisters. Have on hand large Tupperware or Rubbermaid containers.

Soy chocolate chips—Tropical Source soy chocolate is the premier brand used for all the recipes in this book. The chips come in three varieties: semisweet soy chocolate chips, espresso soy chocolate chips, and peanut butter soy chocolate chips. They work beautifully in every cooking procedure and taste delicious. They are organic and sweetened with organic cane juice. If these aren't available, regular chocolate works fine.

Unsweetened cocoa powder—Cocoa powder is made by extracting the cocoa butter from the chocolate liquor, then drying it and grinding it to a powder. Any brand is fine.

Dutch process cocoa—This is a process where an alkaline solution is added to the cocoa powder to make it more uniform in color. The taste is slightly bitter.

GRANULATED SWEETENERS

White sugar—White granulated cane sugar is highly refined sugar-cane juice. It works beautifully in baking and gives the rise and look that we always want in a dessert. The downside is that too much white sugar can be harmful to our bodies. I have recommended some healthier substitutes that work just as well and are easier on the body.

Brown sugar—This is just white sugar with dark cane syrup added to it. It can be used interchangeably with white sugar, but keep in mind the color of the resulting product.

Crystal sugar—This is sugar that is formed into large crystals, and is often used to top baked goods for a little crunch.

Powdered sugar—Also known as confectioners' sugar, this is sugar that is finely ground to a powder with a little cornstarch added to prevent clumping. It is great in certain recipes and for sprinkling on cakes and cookies as a finishing touch.

Light granulated cane juice—Processed by the Florida Crystals Company, this is the best product to use anytime a recipe calls for sugar. It has the consistency of white sugar and works in equal proportions. It is also organic and less processed than commercial sugars.

Dark granulated cane juice—The number one source for this is Sucanat, a brand name that is widely recognized. Use it as a brown-sugar substitute only, because it results in a darker-colored finished product.

The company information for all of these sugar products is included in the Soy Source Guide.

LIQUID SWEETENERS

Honey—Honey is the result of flower nectar that is processed by bees. There is a wide variety of flavors and consistencies of honey, and they are determined by the source of the nectar. The recipes in this book will work well with clover and alfalfa honey. For a richer taste, the darker honey has a stronger flavor. Store all honey in tightly closed jars.

Molasses—This is the liquid portion of the sugarcane that is left over after the sugar has been extracted and refined. Unsulfured molasses is processed during the first stage of sugar extraction and is light and sweet. Sulfured molasses is from the second extraction and is darker and less sweet. Blackstrap molasses is the last extraction, making it very dark and only slightly sweet. Unsulfured is the most commonly used molasses for cooking. Molasses will keep at room temperature for long periods of time.

Maple syrup—Collecting the sap from the trees and boiling it down makes this sweetener into a syrup. Maple syrup can also be used as a flavoring. Make sure you look for "100% maple syrup" on the label. Refrigerate once it is opened to prevent mold.

FLOURS

All-purpose flour—This type of flour is available unbleached and bleached, literally meaning that it has been processed in chlorine bleach. It also has had the bran removed, and most of the nutrition with it. The reason that all-purpose flour is so popular is that it works well in so many cooking procedures. Having been in the business of developing health-oriented recipes for a long time now, I have devised ways to make the less-refined flours work well in baking. I always use unbleached, whole grain flours.

Cake flour—This is very finely milled, bleached white flour.

Whole wheat flour—This flour is ground-up wheat kernels with nothing removed. It has a very coarse consistency. It will work for all types of baking, but the result will be a heavier final product.

Whole wheat pastry flour—This flour is the best of both. It is a little finer ground than the traditional whole wheat flour, but it gives the rise needed for cakes, muffins, and cookies. I use whole wheat pastry flour in all the desserts in this book.

LEAVENING AGENTS AND THICKENERS

Baking soda—Baking soda alone is sodium bicarbonate that breaks down under heat to carbon dioxide. This gas causes baked goods to rise, but the remaining ingredients leave a residue that causes a bitter after-taste. Baking soda should always be used in a mix that has an acidic in-gredient, like cocoa or citrus, to eliminate this problem.

Baking powder—This is made by mixing together baking soda with the necessary amount of acid to avoid the residue aftertaste. Most brands contain aluminum, so buy Rumford Aluminum-Free brand at any market or health food store. Buy it in small quantities so you know you are always using a fresh batch.

Cornstarch—Extracted from the starch of corn kernels, this white powder acts as a thickener. It works quickly, so always stir vigorously when adding cornstarch to a liquid to avoid forming lumps.

DRY GRAINS, NUTS, SEEDS, AND DRIED FRUITS
Buy grains in no larger than 1-pound packages to ensure freshness. Keep a variety of grains on hand at all times, so you will have a lot to work with at a moment's notice. If you buy grains loose, from bulk bins, be sure to inspect the product and store it sealed in a canister or plastic zipper bag for freshness.

Oatmeal—I use quick-cooking oats so that I have a short cooking time, and not too much liquid is absorbed. You can purchase the high-end expensive brands or just get the regular brands in the cereal aisle at the supermarket.

Rice—Rice is used in relatively few dessert recipes. Have on hand a small bag of a few of each type of rice—white, brown, sticky—to add variety to rice pudding or cookies.

Nuts and seeds—There is a wide variety of nuts and seeds used in the recipes, including almonds, walnuts, hazelnuts, pistachio nuts, pine nuts, and soynuts. Any other nuts you would like to substitute for the ones recommended are fine. Try to buy close to the quantity that you need so there isn't a lot left over. Nuts have a high oil content and must be fresh when you bake with them. The best thing to do with leftover nuts is to store them in plastic in the refrigerator. Seeds also should not sit around for too long. I buy poppyseeds and sesame seeds in the smallest package available. Purchase nuts and seeds in small packages: 3- to 6-ounce bags are enough for a recipe, with a little left over for nibbling.

Dried fruits—Raisins, cranberries, apricots, figs, and dates all have a very long shelf life when dried. It is good to purchase them in resealable bags to keep them moist.

Shredded coconut—The shredded, unsweetened variety is best when a recipe calls for coconut. Use it sparingly, because coconut is naturally high in fat and can add unwanted calories to a healthy dessert. It is not necessary to get a specialty brand. Coconut is available in every supermarket.

OILS, EXTRACTS, LIQUEURS, AND COFFEE

Oils—All oils should be used within a maximum period of 6 months. Unsaturated fats, such as vegetable oils, are likely to turn rancid faster than other fats, so buy these items in sizes that you can use within a few months. Oils can be kept at room temperature after opening. Always reseal the containers tightly, as air can promote spoilage. Some types to have on hand are standard vegetable oil (soybean, corn, or canola), walnut oil, hazelnut oil, and peanut oil.

Liquid flavor extracts—Extracts come in such a wide variety of flavors now. Whenever possible, use the pure extract and keep a variety in small bottles along with your seasonings. Vanilla, almond, orange, lemon, peppermint, and anise are a few good flavors to have on hand.

Alcohol and liqueurs—Kahlúa, Amaretto, kirsch, and Frangelico are the most popular liqueurs used in cooking. Peruse the wine and spirits aisle, and you will find that there are a number of fruit-flavored spirits available that you may want to experiment with. Always buy good-quality alcohol because it really makes a difference in the final product. Artificially flavored substitutes pale in comparison to the real thing.

CANNED AND PRESERVED FOOD

Canned goods can be stored for several years, though I recommend using them within 12 months. I put purchased airtight soy milk, such as Vitasoy, and Mori-Nu tofu in this category, as they can be stored, unopened, in the pantry for up to 1 year. I always keep about half a dozen cartons of both the tofu and soy milk in my pantry.

Peaches, pears, pineapple (crushed, diced, or sliced), and pumpkin are must-haves all year long. Fruit spreads and jams essentially keep forever. I always have strawberry, raspberry, and a mixed berry jam available.

Herbs and spices—All dried seasonings and spices should be purchased in small quantities and used within 3 to 4 months. Whole spices stay fresher longer than ground spices: it is a good idea to have a small spice grinder or an extra coffee grinder just for grinding spices. Nutmeg should be bought whole and then grated on a fine grater as needed. Buy small bunches of fresh herbs as needed for specific recipes. They last for a few days in the refrigerator. There are a few commercially available, premade spice mixtures, such as pumpkin pie spice, that are useful and convenient to keep on hand. The commonly used spices that are always good to have on the shelf are cinnamon, cloves (whole and ground), ground ginger, and nutmeg.

Salt—Salt provides a number of advantages in cooking. It acts as a natural preservative, stabilizing the taste and texture of foods and enhancing their flavor. Commercial table salt is highly refined and may contain additives. In recipes that call for salt, use sea salt; it is the most natural and the minerals in it are intact.

PERISHABLES

It is good to keep at least one package of each of the following products in the refrigerator: water-packed tofu, soy cheese, soy cream cheese, and soy yogurt. All of these are sold in refrigerated sections of the market and do not come in aseptically sealed packages. Soy milk or water-packed tofu will keep in the refrigerator and should be consumed within a week. Remember to change the water in water-packed tofu daily to retard spoilage. Soy cheeses can be refrigerated or frozen in their original packages; and cream cheeses, soy yogurt, and soy sour cream should be be used within 2 weeks.

Eggs—Eggs are used very sparingly in this book. Most of the desserts are completely vegetarian, but in certain recipes eggs will make them a lot easier to prepare. Use fresh large eggs, and of course don't use any that have been cracked before you bought them. In most recipes calling for eggs, it is best to have them at room temperature. Leave them out for 30 minutes before mixing, as they will be easier to work with and more liquid.

FREEZER

In the freezer you can keep premade pie shells, ganache, and frostings; even cakes can be frozen for future use. Wrap them very tightly, preferably in airtight plastic bags, and use everything up within 3 months.

KITCHEN EQUIPMENT
Appliances

Electric mixer—A tabletop electric mixer such as a KitchenAid is an excellent investment that will last a lifetime. If you prefer a handheld mixer, get a powerful one that will hold up to a lot of use.

Food processor or blender—These two pieces of equipment are really not considered interchangeable, but in the absence of one, you can use the other. Generally speaking, food processors are great for chopping and for mixing ingredients thoroughly because they have a wide surface area. Blenders are better for pureeing liquids at a high speed. Whether you buy one or both, get good, reliable brands you can trust. You will use them frequently.

Cookware

Cookware is a big investment. You don't have to go out and spend a fortune; just replace whatever is worn out with good-quality pots and pans.

Baking Pans

Always use the size pan that is designated in the recipe. Most good-quality pans and cooking utensils have the size imprinted in them for accuracy and ease of preparation. If you are unsure, measure the pan. All of the pan sizes called for in this book are available at your local supermarket. NordicWare and Easy-Bake are a couple of readily available brands that have almost every shape and size pan used in this book. It couldn't get any easier.

Bundt pan—Traditional bundt pans are usually 10-cup pans, and they are about 12 inches in diameter. All the bundt recipes call for a 6-cup, 8-inch bundt pan. NordicWare makes a terrific nonstick 6-cup pan.

Springform pan—This pan is used for cheesecakes and tarts. It has a spring release so you can remove the side piece from the cake without damage.

Pie pans—These pans are wider at the rim than at the base and are available in shallow and deep-dish varieties in both 8-inch and 9-inch sizes, made from glass or aluminum. Disposable pans are also available.

Angel food cake pans—These pans have high sides and removable bottoms because it is very difficult to remove angel food cake from its baking pan. There are several sizes available.

Aluminum disposable pans—These pans are available in every size imaginable, and they are very convenient if you don't have a lot of storage space.

Muffin tins—All of the muffin recipes in this book make 12 muffins, so just buy a sturdy nonstick or disposable 12-count tin and line it with muffin papers.

Soufflé cups—Have available a 3-ounce and a 5-ounce set of 6 to 8 soufflé cups. This will give you versatility in sizes and portions, especially when entertaining.

Loaf pans—The standard size of domestic loaf pans is 8½ x 4½ inches, and nonstick is best for easy removal of baked goods. When making a larger quantity of cakes, bake 2 loaves rather than 1 large one.

Other Kitchen Supplies

Parchment paper—Parchment paper is great for lining pans and easy removal of cakes. It can be purchased in large quantities or by the roll. Wax paper should never be substituted for parchment. It is not used in baking because the wax will melt into the food.

Cake tester—Professional metal cake testers are easy to find, but you can also use a toothpick or thin wooden skewer. Push the tester all the way into the center of the cake, and make sure it comes out clean before removing the cake from the oven.

Kitchen timers—Start a collection! Every market and gourmet cookware store carries fabulous novelty kitchen timers. Ideally, you should make sure the timer goes to 1 full hour.

Cooling racks—Cooling racks are an absolute necessity and come in a variety of sizes. For the recipes in this book, the small 12-inch tabletop racks are fine. They can hold small cakes or large cookie sheets, are inexpensive, and can be stacked to save room.

Wire whips—Also called wire whisks, these come in handy for many cooking and baking procedures. Buy two or three in each size. They wear quickly, so it is good to have some extras.

Spatulas—Heat-resistant rubber spatulas are the best buy, and the most durable. The plastic spatulas melt and fray easily and do not scrape clean. There are so many colors to choose from, you can coordinate them with your kitchen décor.

Stainless steel mixing bowls—The bowl of choice is stainless steel. You will need a lot of these, so buy at least three sets of four bowls, or buy them individually. They are light and last for years.

Liquid measuring cups—Plastic measuring cups are great because they won't break in the kitchen, and come in a wide variety of sizes. Get a 1-cup, 2-cup, and 4-cup size with both American and metric measurements.

Dry measuring cups—The sturdy stainless steel dry measuring cups are the best. Buy two complete sets to avoid having to wash cups while you are working. It is worth a trip to a specialty cookware store to get the set that has cups in several different sizes.

Measuring spoons—Purchase two sets of stainless steel spoons, with a wide range of graduated measurements.

Basic Preparation Techniques

Calibrating the oven—Have the repairman of your local utilities company come in and check your oven, gas or electric, for safety hazards and proper functioning. Keeping the oven in good working order and calibrated properly will result in successful baked goods.

Doubling a recipe—When you need to accommodate more people, always make two of the same item rather than doubling up on a batter and pouring it in the same pan. Cakes do not always work when scaled up in direct proportion.

Measuring ingredients—Follow the measurements exactly for each and every recipe. They are designed to work in any kitchen, but if you guess at the quantities, you will not get the desired result and will not be able to trace the problem. Also, use the proper cups for what is being measured. Liquid is measured by volume, dry is measured by weight. Measuring cups that are glass or plastic with a spout are used for liquids. Usually, measuring cups that are flatter and made from metal are for measuring dry ingredients. It is also good to have a kitchen scale, so when the weight of an ingredient is listed, there will be no guesswork.

Greasing or lining the pan—There are several ways to grease a pan for baking. The traditional method of spreading butter or margarine on the bottom of the pan works, but it tends to grease unevenly. It is necessary to grease deep pans, such as bundt pans, so the cake is not difficult to remove when cooled. The most popular way of preparing a pan nowadays is with a cooking spray. However, it contains a propellant that may be harmful to the environment. To accomplish the same thing in a much healthier way, get a medium-size spray bottle from the hardware store, fill it with vegetable oil, then spray the pan. The other method of lining the pan is with parchment paper. This works well on very shallow pans and cookie sheets.

Separating eggs into yolks and whites—It is best to separate the eggs when they are cold, and let them sit to room temperature before whipping. It is important that no yolk gets left in the whites, because when whipped separately, egg whites create volume.

Creaming the sugar and margarine or egg yolk—The sugar and fats are creamed together in the electric mixer ahead to create volume and to combine the ingredients thoroughly. The best way to accomplish this is to put the fat in first and gradually add the sugar.

Melting chocolate chips—When melting chocolate, you have to keep a close eye on it. The best way to melt chocolate is over a double boiler, stirring occasionally until it is almost all melted. Remove it from the heat and continue to stir. If you are experienced, you can do it on the stovetop over a low heat, whisking constantly. You must use clean, dry bowls and pans, and not overcook the chocolate to the point of graininess. This will render it useless.

Zesting citrus—Zest refers to the outermost layer of skin of an orange, lemon, or lime. There is a tool called a zester that works by just sliding it along the side of the fruit. You can also use a vegetable peeler, but be gentle so as to avoid cutting through to the white, bitter pith underneath. Cut the zest in ribbonlike strips or mince it with a knife.

Toasting nuts—Preheat the oven to 350°F and spread the nuts on a cookie sheet. Toast for 7 to 10 minutes. Check them at about 5 minutes, and give the cookie sheet a shake. The larger nuts may take a few minutes longer.

Cutting a cake into layers—Wait until the cake is completely cooled before cutting it. Set the cake on a stand or a round piece of cardboard. Use a knife with a long serrated blade, also known as a bread knife, and cut slowly and evenly across the cake.

Frosting—It is best to take a cake-decorating class, but if you want to wing it on your own, here is the best approach: always frost the top first and spread down toward the sides. You can do the final touches after the cake is completely covered in the frosting.

CAKES AND FROSTINGS

I have always loved the art of baking cakes. As a small child with my Susie Homemaker set, I would put my child-sized pans in my mother's oven, and hope for the best. As a teenager, I graduated to boxed cake mixes and canisters of hot pink frosting, and everyone marveled at my abilities. Ironically, I ended up in college majoring in nutrition. Appreciating the value of a more healthful diet, I then went on to culinary school, where I learned a lot about the chemistry of baking, the compatibility of ingredients, and putting together flavor combinations that work. I have since brought together a wide variety of cake-making styles, flavors, and presentations that are great-tasting and great for you, all made with soy!

With all the knowledge I have acquired over the years, I still love the anticipation of waiting for the liquid batter to form miraculously into a luscious, high rise. From a one-layer torte to a multilevel, towering treat, cakes can be easy to make as long as you follow instructions. Baking is a science, and throwing the ingredients together without carefully measuring them can result in a disaster. The added plus of using soy products in cakes doesn't mean skimping on taste and texture. Done properly, the possibilities are endless, and you can mix and match the cakes and frosting for a wide variety of tastes. What these cakes all have in common is delicious-tasting, healthy ingredients that are easy to prepare. In this book I also call for small-sized baking pans to keep the portions under control. Whether baking for yourself, your family, or guests, you will be astounded at the results. From the simple Mango Poppyseed Soy Cake, to the highly decorative Strawberry Soy Layer Cake with Tofu Coconut Cream Frosting, to the simple yet elegant Chocolate Hazelnut Soy Cake with Soy Chocolate Ganache, there is something for every taste and every occasion. Whenever possible, serve the cake first and mention the soy later.

FUDGY CHOCOLATE SOY BUNDT CAKE WITH TOFU CHOCOLATE MOCHA AND VANILLA DRIZZLES

Bundt cakes have an understated beauty, both elegant and comfortable at the same time. They can be used for a special occasion, covered in Tofu Chocolate Mocha and Vanilla Drizzles, or as a great backup for unexpected company or a potluck. In this recipe I call for a 6-cup bundt pan so that the calories and fat are kept to a minimum, without skimping on taste and appearance.

 **MAKES 10 SLICES**

1 cup whole wheat pastry flour

½ cup soy flour

½ teaspoon baking soda

¼ teaspoon salt

6 ounces semisweet soy chocolate chips

2 whole eggs

1 cup sugar or light granulated cane juice

1 teaspoon vanilla extract

1 cup brewed coffee, cold

¼ cup Tofu Chocolate Mocha Drizzle (recipe follows)

¼ cup Tofu Vanilla Drizzle (recipe follows)

1. Preheat the oven to 325°F and lightly grease a 6-cup, nonstick bundt pan.

2. In a mixing bowl, combine the flours, baking soda, and salt. Set aside.

3. Over medium heat in a small saucepan, melt the chocolate chips, stirring continuously with a whisk until the chocolate reaches a thick batterlike consistency. Remove from the heat and set aside.

4. Cream the eggs and sugar, and scrape in the melted chocolate. Add the vanilla, and mix until smooth. Scrape down the sides of the bowl, and add the coffee.

5. Add the chocolate mixture to the flour mixture. Whisk until combined. Pour into the prepared pan, and bake for 1 hour, or until a cake tester comes out clean. Cool for 20 minutes and invert on a platter. Let cool completely before decorating with the drizzles or the frosting of your choice.

After frosting, this cake will keep, wrapped, in the refrigerator for 4 days.

NUTRIENT ANALYSIS

Calories 245 • Protein 6.3 g • Carbohydrate 43 g • Fat 7 g • Fiber 3 g • Cholesterol 42 mg • Sodium 201 mg

BAKING TIPS

Bundt Pans

Cake batters tend to stick to the bottom of bundt pans. Use a bundt pan with a nonstick surface and grease it lightly. This will prevent any sticking.

Soy Chocolate Chips

Soy chocolate chips work beautifully in cooking, baking, and candy making. It is best to melt chocolate in a double boiler, but if you are experienced, you can do it on the stovetop over a low heat.

These multicolored, easy-to-prepare drizzles are a perfect fit for the Fudgy Chocolate Soy Bundt Cake, but can also be used to frost other cakes, cupcakes, and even cookies.

Tofu Chocolate Mocha Drizzle

MAKES ¼ CUP

2 tablespoons regular tofu

1 tablespoon powdered
   sugar

1 tablespoon unsweetened
   cocoa powder

1 tablespoon cold coffee

1 tablespoon soy milk

1. In an electric mixer, combine the tofu, powdered sugar, and cocoa and beat until smooth. Add the coffee and soy milk, and continue just to beat, maintaining a thick consistency.

2. Using a teaspoon, drizzle the chocolate mocha mixture evenly across the top of the bundt cake.

Tofu Vanilla Drizzle

2 tablespoons regular tofu

**2 tablespoons powdered
  sugar**

½ teaspoon vanilla extract

2 tablespoons soy milk

1. In an electric mixer, combine the tofu and powdered sugar and beat until smooth; add the vanilla and soy milk and continue just to beat, maintaining a thick consistency.

2. Using a teaspoon, drizzle the vanilla mixture in stripes over the chocolate mocha drizzle. Serve immediately.

Both of these drizzle mixtures will keep in the refrigerator for up to 1 week.

NUTRIENT ANALYSIS
Calories 15 • Protein 0.6 g • Carbohydrate 2.3 g • Fat 0.3 g • Fiber 0.2 g • Cholesterol 0 • Sodium 1 mg

CHOCOLATE HAZELNUT SOY CAKE
WITH SOY CHOCOLATE GANACHE

This elegant single layer combines the moistness of cake with the velvety smooth, mouth feel of ganache chocolate, and the crunch of hazelnuts. It is one of my favorites for entertaining.

MAKES 10 SLICES

FLAVORING TIPS

Flavored Oils
Oils from nuts will always impart their flavors to the finished product. Each nut is distinctive, and can be used to enhance baked goods and frostings.

Liqueurs
Something as basic as vanilla extract or Frangelico or Grand Marnier will bring out the best in anything it is put in.

1 cup whole wheat pastry flour
½ cup soy flour
1 tablespoon baking soda
1 cup sugar or light granulated cane juice
½ cup unsweetened cocoa powder
1½ cups whole soy milk
1 tablespoon hazelnut oil
1 teaspoon Frangelico (hazelnut liqueur)
1 cup Soy Chocolate Ganache (recipe follows)
¼ cup chopped hazelnuts

1. Preheat the oven to 350°F and grease or line an 8-inch round cake pan.

2. In a large bowl, combine the whole wheat pastry flour, soy flour, baking soda, sugar, and cocoa and set aside.

3. In a separate bowl, combine the soy milk, hazelnut oil, and Frangelico until smooth. Pour the soy milk mixture into the flour mixture, stirring with a wire whisk until well combined.

4. Pour the batter into the greased pan and bake for 30 minutes, or until the cake springs back when touched. Cool completely.

5. Remove the cake from the pan and frost with the ganache. Before the ganache is completely cooled, sprinkle with chopped hazelnuts.

After frosting, this cake will keep, wrapped, in the refrigerator for 1 week.

NUTRIENT ANALYSIS

Calories 270 • Protein 7.2 g • Carbohydrate 44 g • Fat 9 g • Fiber 4.4 g • Cholesterol 0 • Sodium 132 mg

Soy Chocolate Ganache

Soy milk instead of heavy cream makes this velvety ganache as smooth as silk. Use a glass bowl for best results.

1¾ cups (10 ounces) semi-
    sweet soy chocolate
    chips
¾ cup whole soy milk

1. Put the chocolate chips in a medium bowl and set aside.

2. In a small saucepan, heat the soy milk over a medium flame, just until it starts to boil.

3. Remove from the heat and pour directly over the chocolate chips; with a wire whip, mix quickly until smooth.

4. Immediately pour evenly over the cake until it is covered. Let cool and serve.

    This recipe can be made ahead and refrigerated or frozen.

COOKING NOTE

This recipe will coat a two-layer, 8-inch cake. Cut the recipe in half when frosting an 8-inch one-layer cake.

NUTRIENT ANALYSIS FOR 10 SERVINGS
Calories 141 • Protein 1.6 g • Carbohydrate 18 g • Fat 8.8 g • Fiber 2 g • Cholesterol 0 • Sodium 5 mg

POMEGRANATE SOY CAKE WITH SOY CHOCOLATE GANACHE

This brilliant red cake is a great treat for the fall when fresh pomegranates are in season. You can also buy the juice at Middle Eastern specialty groceries or through mail-order sources.

MAKES 10 SLICES

2 whole eggs

¾ cup sugar or light granulated cane juice

½ cup whole wheat pastry flour

½ cup soy flour

1 teaspoon baking powder

1 cup pomegranate juice

1 cup Soy Chocolate Ganache (page 39)

1. Preheat the oven to 350°F. Line or grease an 8-inch cake pan.

2. In a mixing bowl, beat the eggs until foamy and gradually add the sugar. Continue beating until thoroughly combined.

3. Combine the whole wheat pastry flour, soy flour, and baking powder and mix thoroughly. Fold into the egg mixture, alternating with the pomegranate juice. Pour the cake batter into the pan and bake for 40 minutes.

4. Cool for 15 minutes and invert the cake onto a cake frosting rack. Frost with the Soy Chocolate Ganache.

After frosting, this cake will keep, wrapped, in the refrigerator for 3 days.

NUTRIENT ANALYSIS
Calories 193 • Protein 5 g • Carbohydrate 33 g • Fat 5.8 g • Fiber 2.1 g • Cholesterol 42 mg • Sodium 57 mg

SOY YELLOW LAYER CAKE WITH SOY CHOCOLATE CREAM CHEESE FROSTING

This soy creation of basic yellow cake with chocolate frosting is the grandmother of all cakes. Frost with the luscious Soy Chocolate Cream Cheese Frosting, or be creative and use any number of frostings in this chapter. Fancy decorative frosting designs will make it an all-occasion knockout.

1 cup whole wheat pastry flour

1 cup soy flour

2 teaspoons baking powder

$\frac{1}{3}$ cup soft soy margarine

¾ cup sugar or light granulated cane juice

2 whole eggs

¾ cup soy milk

1 teaspoon vanilla extract

½ cup raspberry jam

2 cups Soy Chocolate Cream Cheese Frosting (recipe follows)

1. Preheat the oven to 350°F, and grease and flour two 8-inch cake pans.

2. In a large bowl, combine the whole wheat pastry flour, soy flour, and baking powder and set aside.

3. With an electric mixer, beat the margarine and sugar together until creamy.

4. Add the eggs and beat well; add the soy milk and vanilla and beat until smooth.

5. Gradually add the liquid mixture to the dry ingredients, stirring until thoroughly combined.

6. Pour the batter into the greased pans and bake for 30 minutes.

7. Cool until the cakes reach room temperature. Spread the raspberry jam evenly on one layer and top with the other layer. Frost with the Soy Chocolate Cream Cheese Frosting and serve immediately.

After frosting, this cake will keep, wrapped, in the refrigerator for 3 days.

NUTRIENT ANALYSIS

Calories 380 • Protein 11 g • Carbohydrate 52 g • Fat 15 g • Fiber 4 g • Cholesterol 42 mg • Sodium 157 mg

Soy Chocolate Cream Cheese Frosting

**6 ounces semisweet soy
chocolate chips**

12 ounces firm tofu

4 ounces soy cream cheese

2 cups powdered sugar

1. Over a double boiler, melt the chocolate chips until smooth.

2. In a food processor, puree the tofu, soy cream cheese, and powdered sugar until thoroughly combined.

3. Gradually beat in the melted chocolate chips until the frosting is smooth and fluffy.

4. Chill for 1 hour before frosting, or store in the refrigerator in an airtight container for up to 1 week.

NUTRIENT ANALYSIS

Calories 245 • Protein 6.3 g • Carbohydrate 43 g • Fat 7 g • Fiber 3 g • Cholesterol 42 mg • Sodium 201 mg

FOUR-LAYER SOY YELLOW CHERRY CAKE WITH SOY CHOCOLATE CREAM CHEESE FROSTING

This is the glamorized version of the basic yellow layer cake. I use dried Bing cherries for that extra taste and good looks. Serve the cake on a good silver platter; it gives it an extraordinary appearance.

½ cup whole wheat pastry flour

½ cup soy flour

1 teaspoon baking powder

3 tablespoons soft soy margarine

⅓ cup sugar or light granulated cane juice

1 whole egg

⅓ cup soy milk

½ teaspoon vanilla extract

¾ cup dried Bing cherries

1½ cups Soy Chocolate Cream Cheese Frosting (page 42)

1. Preheat the oven to 350°F and grease and flour an 8-inch square baking pan.

2. In a large bowl, combine the whole wheat pastry flour, soy flour, and baking powder and set aside.

3. With an electric mixer, beat the margarine and sugar together until creamy.

4. Add the egg and beat well; add the soy milk and vanilla and beat until smooth.

5. Gradually add the liquid mixture to the dry ingredients, stirring until thoroughly combined. Fold in the dried cherries.

6. Pour the batter into the greased pan and bake for 25 minutes.

7. Cool until the cake reaches room temperature. Cut the cake in half crosswise, and then through each middle to make 4 layers. Frost with the Soy Chocolate Cream Cheese Frosting and serve immediately.

After frosting, this cake will keep, wrapped, in the refrigerator for 3 days.

NUTRIENT ANALYSIS

Calories 171 • Protein 5 g • Carbohydrate 26 g • Fat 6 g • Fiber 2 g • Cholesterol 21 mg • Sodium 67 mg

MANGO POPPYSEED SOY CAKE

Originally, this recipe was a plain poppyseed cake. While working, I stopped to get a glass of mango juice, and the course of history was changed forever! A wedge of this cake tastes perfect on its own, or with a hot cup of mango tea.

MAKES 10 SLICES

½ cup whole wheat pastry flour

½ cup soy flour

1 teaspoon baking powder

2 whole eggs

¾ cup sugar or light granulated cane juice

1 cup mango juice

1 tablespoon poppyseeds

1. Preheat the oven to 350°F. Line or grease an 8-inch cake pan.

2. In a large mixing bowl, combine the whole wheat pastry flour, soy flour, and baking powder and mix thoroughly.

3. In an electric mixer or food processor, beat the eggs until foamy, and gradually add the sugar and then the mango juice. Continue beating until thoroughly combined.

4. Add the egg mixture to the flour mixture and beat until combined. Fold in the poppyseeds.

5. Pour the cake batter into the pan and bake for 40 minutes.

6. Cool for 20 minutes and invert the cake onto a cooling rack and cool completely.

This cake will keep in the refrigerator, wrapped tightly, for 5 days.

NUTRIENT ANALYSIS
Calories 126 • Protein 4.3 g • Carbohydrate 24 g • Fat 2 g • Fiber 1.8 g • Cholesterol 42 mg • Sodium 59 mg

STRAWBERRY SOY LAYER CAKE WITH TOFU COCONUT CREAM FROSTING

This cake can only be described as heavenly. The slightly pink color of the cake layers is a beautiful contrast to the white frosting and coconut shavings. Since strawberries are readily available, you can whip up this dazzling dream cake all year long.

MAKES 10 SLICES

6 medium strawberries, plus 10 whole medium strawberries, for garnish
1 cup whole wheat pastry flour
1 cup soy flour
2 teaspoons baking powder
1/3 cup soft soy margarine
3/4 cup sugar or light granulated cane juice
1 whole egg
3/4 cup soy milk
1 teaspoon vanilla extract
1/2 cup strawberry jam
1 1/2 cups Tofu Coconut Cream Frosting (recipe follows)

1. Preheat the oven to 350°F and grease and flour two 8-inch cake pans. In the food processor, puree the 6 strawberries and set aside.

2. In a large bowl, combine the flours and baking powder and set aside.

3. With an electric mixer, beat the margarine and sugar together until creamy.

4. Add the egg, beat well; add the strawberry puree, soy milk, and vanilla and beat until smooth.

5. Gradually add the liquid mixture to the dry ingredients, combining well.

6. Pour the batter into the greased pans and bake for 30 minutes.

7. Cool until the cakes reach room temperature. Spread the strawberry jam evenly on one layer and top with the other layer.

8. Frost with the Tofu Coconut Cream Frosting and garnish with the whole strawberries. Serve immediately.

This cake will keep, wrapped, in the refrigerator for 2 days.

NUTRIENT ANALYSIS
Calories 316 • Protein 9 g • Carbohydrate 42 g • Fat 13 g • Fiber 3 g • Cholesterol 21 mg • Sodium 149 mg

Tofu Coconut Cream Frosting

MAKES 1½ CUPS

8 ounces firm tofu

4 ounces soy cream cheese

½ cup powdered sugar

¼ cup shredded, unsweet-
   ened coconut

1. In a food processor, puree the tofu until smooth.

2. Add the soy cream cheese and powdered sugar and beat until thoroughly combined.

3. Add the shredded coconut and mix gently until thoroughly combined.

4. Refrigerate for 1 hour before frosting, or store in the refrigerator in an airtight container for up to 1 week.

NUTRIENT ANALYSIS

Calories 75 • Protein 2.2 g • Carbohydrate 6.3 g • Fat 5 g • Fiber 0 • Cholesterol 0 • Sodium 56 mg

BLOOD ORANGE SOY CAKE WITH ORANGE SOY CREAM CHEESE FROSTING

The inspiration for this cake is the lovely blood orange tree I have in my backyard. The burst of luscious red color of the blood orange pulp is dazzling. If finding blood oranges is difficult, feel free to use any oranges you may have on hand.

 **MAKES 10 SLICES**

1 cup whole wheat pastry
   flour

¼ cup soy flour

1½ teaspoons baking
   powder

1 cup sugar or light granulated cane juice

3 egg yolks

⅓ cup blood orange juice
   (2 whole blood oranges)

3 egg whites

1½ cups Blood Orange Soy
   Cream Cheese Frosting
   (recipe follows)

1 whole blood orange, sliced
   thin

1. Preheat the oven to 350°F. Lightly grease or line with parchment paper two 8-inch round cake pans.

2. In a mixing bowl, combine the whole wheat pastry flour, soy flour, baking powder, and sugar, mix well, and set aside.

3. In an electric mixer, beat the egg yolks thoroughly, add the orange juice, and blend.

4. Add the egg yolk mixture to the flour mixture and mix thoroughly.

5. In the electric mixer or by hand, beat the egg whites until stiff and fold into the flour mixture until fully combined.

6. Pour into the prepared pans and bake for 25 minutes, or until a cake tester comes out clean.

7. Cool completely before removing from the pan. Frost with the Blood Orange Soy Cream Cheese Frosting and garnish with the orange slices. Serve immediately.

After frosting, this cake will keep, wrapped, in the refrigerator for 1 week.

NUTRIENT ANALYSIS
Calories 230 • Protein 7 g • Carbohydrate 39 g • Fat 6 g • Fiber 2 g • Cholesterol 63 mg • Sodium 125 mg

Citrus zest—the colorful part of the skin of the fruit—adds strong flavor to dressings, baked goods, and other foods. There are a few tricks to removing the zest properly, however, since the white pith just underneath the zest is very bitter.

• One technique is to use a special tool called a zester, which peels away thin ribbons of colored zest and leaves behind the pith. Mince these ribbons finely or leave them intact for decorative garnishes.

• Another technique is to use a vegetable peeler and carefully scrape away just the zest. Mince the zest finely with a sharp knife.

Blood Orange Soy Cream Cheese Frosting

MAKES 1½ CUPS

COOKING NOTE

Any oranges that you have on hand can be used in this recipe

8 ounces firm tofu
4 ounces soy cream cheese
½ cup powdered sugar
Zest and juice of 1 medium
    blood orange

1. In a food processor, puree the tofu until smooth.

2. Add the soy cream cheese and powdered sugar and beat until thoroughly combined.

3. Add the orange zest and juice and mix gently until thoroughly combined.

4. Refrigerate for 1 hour before frosting, or store in the refrigerator in an airtight container for up to 1 week.

To assemble, spread frosting on the top of the first layer, and top with the second layer. Cover the whole cake with frosting and garnish with orange slices.

NUTRIENT ANALYSIS
Calories 75 • Protein 2.3 g • Carbohydrate 7.5 g • Fat 4 g • Fiber 0 • Cholesterol 0 • Sodium 55 mg

CHOCOLATE MAPLE SOY CAKE WITH CHOCOLATE ALMOND SOY FROSTING

Always use pure Vermont maple syrup in this recipe. This cake has assertive flavors and should be showcased. The rich sweetness of pure maple syrup is complemented by the Chocolate Almond Soy Frosting.

MAKES 10 SLICES

½ cup whole wheat pastry flour

½ cup soy flour

⅓ cup unsweetened cocoa powder

1 teaspoon baking soda

⅛ teaspoon salt

8 ounces firm tofu

¾ cup sugar or light granulated cane juice

2 tablespoons maple syrup

¼ cup warm water

2 tablespoons soybean oil

1 whole egg

2 teaspoons vanilla extract

½ cup Chocolate Almond Soy Frosting (recipe follows)

¼ cup slivered almonds

1. Preheat the oven to 350°F. Lightly grease an 8-inch round cake pan.

2. In a mixing bowl, combine the whole wheat pastry flour, soy flour, cocoa, baking soda, and salt. Mix until thoroughly combined.

3. In a food processor, puree the tofu until smooth. Add the sugar, maple syrup, water, soybean oil, egg, and vanilla. Continue to process until smooth.

4. Add the tofu mixture to the flour mixture and beat until combined. Pour the mixture into the prepared cake pan and bake for 30 minutes. Cool completely.

5. Frost with the Chocolate Almond Soy Frosting and sprinkle the slivered almonds on top.

This cake will keep, wrapped, in the refrigerator for 2 days.

NUTRIENT ANALYSIS

Calories 243 • Protein 8 g • Carbohydrate 38 g • Fat 6 g • Fiber 4 g • Cholesterol 21 mg • Sodium 169 mg

Chocolate Almond Soy Frosting

MAKES ½ CUP

NOTE ABOUT OILS

Soybean oil works great in baking! For a flavor variety or enhancement, use walnut or hazelnut oil.

COOKING NOTE

The Chocolate Almond Soy Frosting goes on as a light, thin coat on this cake and is sprinkled with slivered almonds.

½ cup whole soy milk

2 tablespoons almond extract

1 cup unsweetened cocoa powder

1 cup powdered sugar

In a food processor or electric mixer, combine all the ingredients and beat until smooth. Frost the cake immediately, or store the mix in the refrigerator for 1 week.

NUTRIENT ANALYSIS
Calories 80 • Protein 2.2 g • Carbohydrate 14 g • Fat 0.9 g • Fiber 2.4 g • Cholesterol 0 • Sodium 5.7 mg

CHOCOLATE LAYER SOY CAKE WITH CHOCOLATE SOYNUT BUTTER FROSTING

This soy-enhanced chocolate cake is a memorable experience when joined with the Chocolate Soynut Butter Frosting. Chocolate and soynut butter, which is like peanut butter, is the most comforting food combination I know.

MAKES 10 SLICES

1 cup whole wheat pastry flour

½ cup soy flour

1 tablespoon baking soda

1 cup sugar or light granulated cane juice

½ cup unsweetened cocoa powder

1½ cups whole soy milk

1 tablespoon vegetable oil

1 teaspoon vanilla extract

2½ cups Chocolate Soynut Butter Frosting (recipe follows)

¼ cup chopped soynuts

1. Preheat the oven to 350°F and grease an 8-inch round cake pan.

2. In a large bowl, combine the whole wheat pastry flour, soy flour, baking soda, sugar, and cocoa and set aside.

3. In a separate bowl, combine the soy milk, vegetable oil, and vanilla until smooth. Pour the soy milk mixture into the flour mixture, stirring with a wire whisk until well combined.

4. Pour the batter into the greased pan and bake for 30 minutes, or until the cake springs back when touched. Cool completely.

5. Remove from the pan and frost with the Chocolate Soynut Butter Frosting. Sprinkle with the soynuts and serve.

After frosting, this cake will keep, wrapped, in the refrigerator for at least a week.

NUTRIENT ANALYSIS

Calories 255 • Protein 8.4 g • Carbohydrate 46 g • Fat 4.6 g • Fiber 6 g • Cholesterol 0 • Sodium 396 mg

Chocolate Soynut Butter Frosting

MAKES 2½ CUPS

**1 cup unsweetened cocoa
   powder**
1 cup powdered sugar
½ cup whole soy milk
1 tablespoon soynut butter
1 teaspoon vanilla extract

In a food processor or electric mixer, combine all the ingredients and beat until smooth. Frost the cake immediately, or store the mix in the refrigerator for 1 week.

NUTRIENT ANALYSIS
Calories 75 • Protein 2.3 g • Carbohydrate 7.5 g • Fat 4 g • Fiber 0 • Cholesterol 0 • Sodium 55 mg

"NEW YORK" TOFU CHEESECAKE

My all-time favorite dessert is New York cheesecake, and I have been making it from scratch for twenty-five years. Substituting tofu for eggs and using soy cream cheese and organic sweeteners, this recipe has been transformed. These changes take nothing away from the satisfying appeal that this cake is famous for, and the preparation is a breeze.

MAKES 12 SLICES

One 9-inch springform
   Graham Cracker Crust
   (recipe follows)
1½ pounds soft tofu
1 cup sugar or light granulated cane juice
8 ounces soy cream cheese
1 teaspoon vanilla extract

1. Prepare the Graham Cracker Crust ahead and set aside. Preheat the oven to 350°F.

2. In a blender or food processor, puree the tofu until smooth. Add the sugar, soy cream cheese, and vanilla, processing until smooth.

3. Pour the tofu mixture into the prepared crust and bake for 50 minutes.

4. Turn the oven off, leaving the cake in the oven for 1 hour. Remove and cool.

5. Refrigerate the cheesecake overnight. Serve at room temperature.

BAKING TIPS

Cheesecake has a custardlike consistency and requires a long baking and cooling time. For best results, refrigerate the cheesecake overnight and serve the next day.

Cheesecake will keep, wrapped, in the refrigerator for 1 week.

COOKING NOTE

Eight ounces of soy cream cheese is the equivalent of 1 cup. The batter for all of the cheesecake recipes in this book will fill two 9-inch storebought graham cracker piecrusts.

NUTRIENT ANALYSIS
Calories 257 • Protein 6 g • Carbohydrate 29 g • Fat 13 g • Fiber 0 • Cholesterol 0 • Sodium 134 mg

Graham Cracker Crust

With their crumbly cookielike consistency, graham crackers are the most traditional choice for cheesecake crust. This recipe can also be used for a variety of pies. For a change of pace, use the chocolate-flavored graham crackers.

MAKES ONE 9-INCH CRUST OR 6 INDIVIDUAL 3-INCH TART SHELLS

COOKING NOTE

Whole graham crackers come packaged with about 11 whole crackers to a package.

1¼ cups, or 1 package, low-fat graham cracker crumbs

6 tablespoons soft soy margarine

One 9-inch springform pan or 9-inch pie pan, nonstick

1. Process the graham crackers in a food processor on high speed until they are finely ground.

2. Add the margarine and pulse until the mixture reaches the consistency of coarse crumbs.

3. Pat the mixture into a thick layer in the bottom of the springform pan. Fill and bake according to recipe instructions.

NUTRIENT ANALYSIS

Calories 100 • Protein 1 g • Carbohydrate 29 g • Fat 11 g • Fiber 0 • Cholesterol 0 • Sodium 43 mg

CAPPUCCINO CINNAMON TOFU CHEESECAKE

Coffee and cinnamon are strong flavors that go hand in hand, especially when combined with the creamy consistency of this cheesecake. Sprinkle the cake with chocolate-covered espresso beans for some added zip.

One 9-inch springform
   Graham Cracker Crust
   (page 54)
1½ pounds soft tofu
1 cup sugar or light granulated cane juice
8 ounces soy cream cheese
⅓ cup fresh-brewed espresso
   or strong coffee, cooled
1 teaspoon ground cinnamon

1. Prepare the Graham Cracker Crust and set aside. Preheat the oven to 350°F.

2. In a blender or food processor, puree the tofu until smooth. Add the sugar, soy cream cheese, espresso, and cinnamon and process until smooth.

3. Pour the tofu mixture into the prepared crust and bake for 50 minutes.

4. Turn the oven off, leaving the cake in the oven for 1 hour. Remove and cool.

Refrigerate the cheesecake overnight and serve at room temperature.

NUTRIENT ANALYSIS
Calories 258 • Protein 6 g • Carbohydrate 29 g • Fat 13 g • Fiber 0 • Cholesterol 0 • Sodium 134 mg

ORANGE CHOCOLATE CHIP TOFU CHEESECAKE

The cool citrusy flavor and rich creamy texture of this tofu cheesecake makes it taste like a Creamsicle with chocolate chips.

MAKES 12 SLICES

COOKING NOTE

For a little extra orange, spread a light layer of orange marmalade (about ¼ cup) on top of the cheesecake before garnishing.

One 9-inch springform
   Graham Cracker Crust
   (page 54)
1½ pounds soft tofu
1 cup sugar or light granulated cane juice
8 ounces soy cream cheese
3 tablespoons orange extract
¼ cup semisweet soy chocolate chips
Zest of 1 large orange, for
   garnish
¼ cup semisweet soy chocolate chips, for garnish

1. Prepare the Graham Cracker Crust ahead and set aside. Preheat the oven to 350°F.

2. In a blender or food processor, puree the tofu until smooth. Add the sugar, soy cream cheese, and orange extract; process until smooth. Fold in the chocolate chips.

3. Pour the tofu mixture into the prepared crust and bake for 50 minutes.

4. Turn the oven off, leaving the cake in the oven for 1 hour. Remove and cool.

Refrigerate the cheesecake overnight, and serve at room temperature. Garnish with orange zest and chocolate chips.

NUTRIENT ANALYSIS

Calories 293 • Protein 6 g • Carbohydrate 36 g • Fat 14 g • Fiber 0 • Cholesterol 0 • Sodium 138 mg

RASPBERRY MARBLE TOFU CHEESECAKE

This is a golden opportunity to use your decorative talents. The number of different patterns you can make in the cheesecake with the raspberry jam is endless. When entertaining, make two cakes and top with two different flavors of berry jams.

One 9-inch springform
   Graham Cracker Crust
   (page 54)
1½ pounds soft tofu
1 cup sugar or light granulated cane juice
8 ounces soy cream cheese
½ cup raspberry jam
Raspberry Sauce (recipe
   follows)

1. Prepare the Graham Cracker Crust and set aside. Preheat the oven to 350°F.

2. In a blender or food processor, puree the tofu until smooth. Add the sugar and soy cream cheese and process until smooth.

3. Heat the raspberry jam in a small saucepan and whisk until smooth, about 3 minutes.

4. Pour half of the tofu mixture into the prepared crust and drizzle ¼ cup of the raspberry jam over the mix.

5. Cover with the remaining tofu batter and drizzle the remaining jam over the top of the cake. With a toothpick, draw stripes across the jam to create a marbleized pattern.

6. Bake for 50 minutes. Turn the oven off, leaving the cake in the oven for 1 hour. Remove and cool.

Refrigerate the cheesecake overnight. Garnish with fresh raspberries and serve at room temperature with the Raspberry Sauce.

> **COOKING NOTE**
> For variety, any jam and fresh berries in season can be used for a garnish.

NUTRIENT ANALYSIS
Calories 272 • Protein 6 g • Carbohydrate 33 g • Fat 13 g • Fiber 1 g • Cholesterol 0 • Sodium 134 mg

Raspberry Sauce for Plate Decorating

Poured over the cake or just spread on the plate, this sauce is a simple recipe that gives the proper consistency for decorating dessert plates.

½ cup seedless raspberry
jam

3 tablespoons lemon juice

1. In a small saucepan, heat the jam and lemon juice, whisking continuously for 2 minutes.

2. Remove from the heat and spread on a plate.

3. Let cool and serve each slice of Raspberry Marble Tofu Cheesecake (page 57) with some sauce.

NUTRIENT ANALYSIS

Calories 38 • Protein 0.2 g • Carbohydrate 10 g • Fat 0 • Fiber 0.8 g • Cholesterol 0 • Sodium 5 mg

MINIATURE PEACH UPSIDE-DOWN SOY CAKES

Traditional upside-down cakes are famous for the gooey butter and sugar mixture that the fruit caramelizes in when baking. In this version the peaches are baked into individual cakes and topped with a little maple syrup. The taste is incredibly light and sweet.

MAKES 6 MINIATURE CAKES

6 miniature nonstick bundt pans

One 15-ounce can peaches, drained and chopped

1 cup whole wheat pastry flour

1 cup soy flour

2 teaspoons baking powder

1/3 cup soft soy margarine

3/4 cup sugar or light granulated cane juice

2 whole eggs

3/4 cup soy milk

1 teaspoon vanilla extract

6 tablespoons maple syrup

1. Preheat the oven to 350°F. Lightly grease the miniature bundt pans.

2. Place the chopped peaches evenly into the bottom of the pans.

3. In a large bowl, combine the whole wheat pastry flour, soy flour, and baking powder and set aside.

4. In an electric mixer, beat the margarine and sugar together until creamy.

5. Add the eggs and beat well; add the soy milk and vanilla and beat until smooth.

6. Gradually add the liquid mixture to the dry ingredients, stirring until thoroughly combined.

7. Pour the batter into the peach-filled, greased pans and bake for 30 minutes.

8. Cool for 10 minutes and invert the pans.

9. Remove the cakes and cool completely.

10. Drizzle with the maple syrup and serve immediately.

These miniature cakes will keep, wrapped in plastic, for 3 days.

NUTRIENT ANALYSIS
Calories 191.5 • Protein 6.5 g • Carbohydrate 28 g • Fat 7 g • Fiber 3 g • Cholesterol 35 mg • Sodium 85 mg

SOY ANGEL FOOD CAKE

Known for its light, fluffy consistency, angel food cake evokes images of angels resting on clouds in the sky. Even with the soy flour, I managed to get a rise out of this one. Garnish with fresh berries in season.

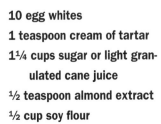

MAKES 12 SLICES, OR 6 INDIVIDUAL CAKES

10 egg whites

1 teaspoon cream of tartar

1¼ cups sugar or light granulated cane juice

½ teaspoon almond extract

½ cup soy flour

½ cup whole wheat pastry flour

1. Preheat the oven to 350°F. Lightly grease a 6-cup angel food pan, or 6 individual pans with removable bottoms.

2. With a hand mixer, beat the egg whites with the cream of tartar until stiff. Gradually add the sugar and almond extract.

3. Mix the flours in a separate bowl and then fold into the egg white mixture.

4. Pour into the angel food pan and bake for 45 minutes. Cool for 10 minutes and turn the cake onto a cooling rack. Cool completely before using.

The cake can be stored in a plastic bag at room temperature for 3 days.

NUTRIENT ANALYSIS FOR 12 SLICES

Calories 123 • Protein 5 g • Carbohydrate 25 g • Fat 0.3 g • Fiber 1 g • Cholesterol 0 • Sodium 143 mg

MINI SOY CHOCOLATE ANGEL FOOD CAKES

These individual cakes are a great way to serve the chocolate version of the light, fluffy Soy Angel Food Cake. Garnish with Soy Chocolate Sauce, fresh fruit, and nuts.

10 egg whites

1 teaspoon cream of tartar

1½ cups sugar or light granulated cane juice

½ cup soy flour

½ cup whole wheat pastry flour

⅓ cup unsweetened cocoa powder

1. Preheat the oven to 350°F. Lightly grease a 6-cup angel food pan or 6 individual pans with removable bottoms.

2. With an electric mixer, beat the egg whites with the cream of tartar until stiff. Gradually add the sugar.

3. Mix the soy flour and pastry flour and the cocoa in a separate bowl and then fold into the egg white mixture.

4. Pour the mix into each pan, filling them about three-quarters full.

5. Bake for 25 minutes. Cool for 10 minutes and turn the cakes onto a cooling rack. Cool completely before removing.

Can be stored in a plastic bag at room temperature for 3 days.

NUTRIENT ANALYSIS FOR 6 CAKES

Calories 311 • Protein 11 g • Carbohydrate 59 g • Fat 4.8 g • Fiber 2.8 g • Cholesterol 0 • Sodium 95 mg

PIES AND TARTS

Good old American classics, pies and tarts—timeless, seasonless, and endless in their appeal. Pies and tarts are differentiated in a few ways. Pies tend to be deep and brimming with filling. They have a flaky crust, which works because the pie is served directly from the pie plate. Tarts are more shallow and should have a stronger crust because they are removed from the pan after baking.

It is a labor of love to prepare a pie or a tart, yet it can be an indulgence and a comfort food, all at once. You can fill pies and tarts with almost anything, and using soy as a base for crusts and for fillings, the possibilities are endless. When I give cooking classes and lectures on the attributes of soy, and how to substitute ingredients, I always feel I have to apologize in advance for taking butter out of the crust and cream out of the fillings. Instead of viewing this as deprivation, it should be cause for celebration. Here is a way of enjoying the foods we love, and taking care of our hearts as well. Many of the fillings in these pie and tart recipes, such as Tofu Coconut Cream Pie, Soynut Pecan Pie, and Tofu Lemon Tartlets with Soynut Tartlet Crust, are based on traditional recipes that are high in calories, fat, and cholesterol. Just a few minor changes using soy products maintains the taste and the luscious mouth feel, along with making these desserts a healthful pleasure. There is no shame in buying storebought crusts and tart shells, and fillings such as the Tofu Custard Pie with Cherry Kiwi Topping and the Tofu Chocolate Fig Tart work well in premade 9-inch whole crusts, as well as in premade 3-inch individual tart shells. Feel free to interchange the different fillings and toppings to suit your own tastes.

TOFU COCONUT CREAM PIE

My husband challenged me to make a soy version of his favorite dessert, coconut cream pie. I whipped this up, and after one taste, he fell in love with me all over again.

MAKES 12 SLICES

One 9-inch Graham Cracker
    Crust (page 54)
1 pound firm tofu
¼ cup brown sugar, tightly
    packed
4 tablespoons shredded,
    unsweetened coconut

1. Preheat the oven to 350°F. Prepare the crust according to the recipe and bake for 15 minutes; let cool.

2. In a food processor or blender on medium speed, puree the tofu until smooth.

3. Add the brown sugar and continue blending until thoroughly combined. Scrape down the sides of the bowl if necessary.

4. Turn the processor on high and add 3 tablespoons of the shredded coconut. Blend for 10 seconds. Pour the mixture into the prepared piecrust and top with the remaining coconut. Refrigerate, covered, for 2 hours or overnight. Serve chilled. Will keep in the refrigerator for 1 week.

COOKING NOTE
Toast the shredded coconut for topping to add extra flavor.

NUTRIENT ANALYSIS
Calories 180 • Protein 4.7 g • Carbohydrate 22 g • Fat 8 g • Fiber 0.7 g • Cholesterol 0 • Sodium 142 mg

TOFU PEAR PIE

This pear-filled, ginger-scented tofu pie is as delicious to look at as it is to eat. It is just perfect for a fall Sunday brunch, when the Bosc pears are ripe and in season. Top with crunchy Soynut Granola for an extra-hearty bite.

MAKES 10 SLICES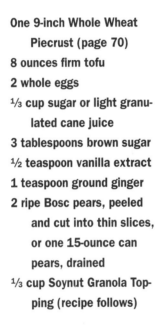

One 9-inch Whole Wheat
   Piecrust (page 70)
8 ounces firm tofu
2 whole eggs
⅓ cup sugar or light granulated cane juice
3 tablespoons brown sugar
½ teaspoon vanilla extract
1 teaspoon ground ginger
2 ripe Bosc pears, peeled
   and cut into thin slices,
   or one 15-ounce can
   pears, drained
⅓ cup Soynut Granola Top-
   ping (recipe follows)

1. Preheat the oven to 375°F. Prepare the piecrust and bake on a cookie sheet for 10 minutes, remove, and cool.

2. In a food processor, puree the tofu until smooth, about 3 minutes. Add the eggs, sugar, brown sugar, vanilla, and ginger and continue to puree until thoroughly combined.

3. Arrange the pear slices in two overlapping circles on the bottom of the prepared pie shell. Pour the tofu mixture over the pears and sprinkle with the Soynut Granola.

4. Bake for 40 minutes, or until the crust is golden brown. Cool completely before serving.

NUTRIENT ANALYSIS

Calories 248 • Protein 6.9 g • Carbohydrate 30 g • Fat 12 g • Fiber 4 g • Cholesterol 42 mg • Sodium 20 mg

Soynut Granola Topping

This crunchy assortment of fruit, grains, and soynuts makes a wonderful topping for pies and ice cream, yet it can stand alone as an instant snack or breakfast cereal.

1 cup assorted pitted, dried
    fruits (apples, apricots,
    pineapple, raisins, and
    dates)
⅓ cup honey
2 teaspoons soybean oil
½ teaspoon almond extract
2 cups old-fashioned rolled
    oats
⅓ cup wheat germ
⅓ cup oat bran
⅓ cup soynuts

1. Preheat the oven to 350°F and line a baking sheet with parchment paper. Coarsely chop the dried fruits and set aside.

2. In a large mixing bowl, with a wire whip, whisk the honey, soybean oil, and almond extract together until thoroughly combined. Add the rolled oats, wheat germ, oat bran, and soynuts, mixing well.

3. Spread the mixture on the baking sheet and cook for 20 minutes. Remove from the oven. When the mixture has cooled completely, add the chopped dried fruits. Can be used as a topping on cakes, pies, and ice cream.

NUTRIENT ANALYSIS
Calories 151 • Protein 5.1 g • Carbohydrate 28 g • Fat 2.9 g • Fiber 3.4 g • Cholesterol 0 • Sodium 2.9 mg

WHOLE WHEAT PIECRUST

This piecrust has a personality of its own, independent of the filling you put in it. Butter is responsible for the flakiness of a crust, and so I used the next best thing, nonhydrogenated margarine. It works like a charm every time.

**MAKES ONE
8-INCH REGULAR
PIECRUST OR ONE
9-INCH DEEP-DISH
PIECRUST OR
SIX 4-INCH
INDIVIDUAL
PIECRUSTS**

2 cups whole wheat pastry
   flour
½ cup soft soy margarine,
   chilled
⅓ cup ice-cold water

1. In a large mixing bowl, combine the flour and the margarine.

2. Using your fingers, work the ingredients together quickly until the mixture resembles coarse flakes.

3. Add the cold water gradually and mix until the dough reaches a lumpy consistency and holds together. Be careful not to overmix or the crust will be tough. Gather it into a ball and flatten it out.

4. Cover the dough in plastic wrap and refrigerate for at least 1 hour or overnight.

5. Roll out the dough to ⅛-inch thickness.

6. Line the pie plate with the dough, crimping the edges decoratively.

7. Bake at 350°F for 10 minutes, or until slightly golden.

NUTRIENT ANALYSIS
Calories 162 • Protein 3.3 g • Carbohydrate 17 g • Fat 9.5 g • Fiber 3 g • Cholesterol 0 • Sodium 5 mg

SOY CARROT GINGER PIE

The subtle sweetness of carrots and the liveliness of the ginger transform this homey-looking pie into a superstar. Not only is the soy advantageous, but the carrots make it chock-full of vitamins and antioxidants.

One 9-inch deep-dish Whole Wheat Piecrust (page 70)

One 14-ounce can cooked carrots

2 whole eggs

1 cup dark brown sugar or dark granulated cane juice

1 teaspoon ground ginger

1 teaspoon ground cinnamon

⅛ teaspoon ground nutmeg

⅓ cup soy milk

⅓ cup soy yogurt

⅓ cup orange juice

1. Preheat the oven to 350°F. Bake the piecrust for 6 minutes before filling.

2. In a food processor, puree the carrots until smooth. Add the eggs and puree until they are fully incorporated.

3. One at a time, add the brown sugar, ginger, cinnamon, nutmeg, soy milk, soy yogurt, and orange juice. Mix thoroughly.

4. Pour into the prepared piecrust and bake for 1 hour. Cool completely before serving.

NUTRIENT ANALYSIS

Calories 244 • Protein 5.7 g • Carbohydrate 33 g • Fat 11 g • Fiber 4 g • Cholesterol 42 mg • Sodium 39 mg

TOFU PUMPKIN PIE

If you only have one tofu dessert at Thanksgiving, make it this one. Prepare more than one because your guests will want seconds, thirds, and fourths. This recipe calls for canned pumpkin, which is always available, and a storebought crust will save you time.

MAKES 10 SLICES

One 9-inch deep-dish Whole
    Wheat Piecrust (page
    70)
1½ pounds firm tofu
1½ cups cooked, canned
    pumpkin
¾ cup brown sugar or dark
    granulated cane juice
1 teaspoon ground cinnamon
½ teaspoon ground ginger
¼ teaspoon ground nutmeg
¼ teaspoon ground cloves

1. Preheat the oven to 350°F. Bake the piecrust for 10 minutes and cool.

2. Put the tofu in the blender and puree until smooth. Add the pumpkin, brown sugar, cinnamon, ginger, nutmeg, and cloves and continue to mix until all ingredients are thoroughly combined.

3. Pour the mixture into the piecrust and bake for 1 hour. Cool and serve warm or at room temperature.

NUTRIENT ANALYSIS
Calories 273 • Protein 10 g • Carbohydrate 32 g • Fat 12 g • Fiber 4.3 g • Cholesterol 0 • Sodium 16 mg

SOYNUT PECAN PIE

An all-American classic is given a healthy twist by incorporating soynuts into the filling. Baking whole nuts in the oven will actually toast them, which brings out the flavor and a heavenly aroma. To top it all off, serve with a scoop of Soynut Tofu Ice Cream (page 148).

MAKES 10 PIECES

One 9-inch deep-dish Whole
   Wheat Piecrust (page
   70)
3 whole eggs
1 cup sugar or light granulated cane juice
½ teaspoon salt
⅓ cup soft soy margarine
⅓ cup light corn syrup
⅓ cup dark corn syrup
1 teaspoon vanilla extract
¾ cup soynuts
¼ cup pecans

1. Preheat the oven to 350°F. Bake the piecrust for 6 minutes before filling.

2. In a large mixing bowl, beat the eggs just until frothy.

3. One at a time, add the sugar, salt, margarine, both corn syrups, and vanilla; mix thoroughly.

4. Fold in the soynuts and pecans and pour into the prepared piecrust. Bake for 1 hour. Cool completely before serving.

NUTRIENT ANALYSIS

Calories 395 • Protein 5.9 g • Carbohydrate 54 g • Fat 18 g • Fiber 3 g • Cholesterol 63 mg • Sodium 188 mg

TOFU CUSTARD PIE WITH CHERRY KIWI TOPPING

This gorgeous, yet simple pie got rave reviews during the taste-testing process. Its creamy rich consistency is complemented by the sweet fruit, and it is beautiful to look at, too.

MAKES 10 SLICES

COOKING NOTE

The custard filling will fill only ⅞ of the pie shell. This leaves enough room to top the pie with cherries and kiwi without any spilling over.

One 9-inch Graham Cracker Crust (page 54)

12 ounces firm tofu

4 ounces soy cream cheese

½ cup sugar or light granulated cane juice

2 teaspoons lemon extract

1 cup canned cherry pie filling

2 kiwi, cut into 10 thin slices right before serving

1. Preheat the oven to 350°F. Prepare the Graham Cracker Crust and bake for 6 minutes; set aside.

2. In a food processor, combine, one at a time, the tofu, soy cream cheese, sugar, and lemon extract and puree until smooth.

3. Pour into the prepared piecrust and bake for 20 minutes. Remove from the oven and cool completely. Refrigerate for at least an hour or overnight.

4. Spread the cherry filling over the pie right before serving. Garnish each piece with 1 slice of kiwi.

This pie will keep, wrapped, in the refrigerator for 5 days.

NUTRIENT ANALYSIS

Calories 249 • Protein 4.1 g • Carbohydrate 36 g • Fat 10 g • Fiber 1.4 g • Cholesterol 0 • Sodium 205 mg

---

CHOCOLATE SOY CREAM PIE

If you crave the chocolate cream pie of your childhood, you'll love this soy remake. The creaminess that the tofu and soy cream cheese provide, combined with semisweet soy chocolate chips, makes a luxurious filling for the chocolate cookie crust.

MAKES 10 SLICES

One 9-inch Graham Cracker Crust made with chocolate graham crackers (page 54)

½ cup semisweet soy chocolate chips

2 tablespoons soy milk

12 ounces firm tofu

4 ounces soy cream cheese

½ cup sugar or light granulated cane juice

1 cup Soy Cream Pie Topping (recipe follows)

¼ cup soynuts (optional)

¼ cup soy espresso chocolate chips (optional)

1. Preheat the oven to 350°F. Prepare the chocolate graham cracker crust and bake for 6 minutes; set aside.

2. In a small saucepan, over medium heat, melt the chocolate chips with the soy milk, whisking continuously until smooth. Set aside.

3. In a food processor, combine the tofu, soy cream cheese, and sugar and puree until smooth. Add the chocolate–soy milk mixture and continue to puree until fully combined.

4. Pour into the prepared piecrust and bake for 20 minutes. Remove from the oven and cool completely. Refrigerate for at least an hour or overnight.

5. Spread the Soy Cream Pie Topping evenly over the pie and serve. Garnish each piece with soynuts or chocolate chips, if desired.

This pie will keep, wrapped, in the refrigerator for 5 days.

COOKING NOTE
This custard filling will fill only ⅞ of the pie shell. This leaves enough room to top the pie with the soy cream evenly.

NUTRIENT ANALYSIS
Calories 304 • Protein 5.4 g • Carbohydrate 37 g • Fat 16 g • Fiber 1.4 g • Cholesterol 0 • Sodium 261 mg

SOY CREAM PIE TOPPING

MAKES 1 CUP

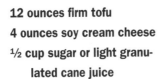

12 ounces firm tofu

4 ounces soy cream cheese

**½ cup sugar or light granu-
lated cane juice**

1. In a food processor, combine the tofu, soy cream cheese, and sugar. Puree until smooth.

2. Refrigerate in an airtight container until ready to use.

This will last a week in the refrigerator.

NUTRIENT ANALYSIS

Calories 57 • Protein 1.1 g • Carbohydrate 5.4 g • Fat 3.4 g • Fiber 0.1 g • Cholesterol 0 • Sodium 57 mg

TROPICAL BANANA SOY CREAM PIE WITH PINEAPPLE AND MACADAMIA NUTS

I just love Hawaii. Every time I go there, I gorge on fresh pineapple and macadamia nuts. To re-create these flavors, and keep the nutritional values from skyrocketing, I lightly top a tofu custard with these tropical delicacies.

MAKES 10 SLICES

One 9-inch Graham Cracker Crust (page 54)
12 ounces firm tofu
4 ounces soy cream cheese
½ cup sugar or light granulated cane juice
1 banana, preferably very ripe
¼ cup dried pineapple, chopped coarsely
¼ cup macadamia nuts, chopped coarsely

1. Preheat the oven to 350°F. Prepare the Graham Cracker Crust and bake for 6 minutes; set aside.

2. In a food processor, combine the tofu, soy cream cheese, and sugar and puree until smooth. Add the banana and continue to puree until fully combined.

3. Pour into the prepared piecrust and spread the dried pineapple and macadamia nuts evenly across the top of the pie.

4. Bake for 20 minutes. Remove from the oven and cool completely. Refrigerate for at least an hour or overnight.

This pie will keep, wrapped, in the refrigerator for 5 days.

> **COOKING NOTE**
> This custard filling will fill only ⅞ of the pie shell. This leaves enough room to decorate the pie with the dried pineapple and macadamia nuts.

NUTRIENT ANALYSIS
Calories 256 • Protein 4.2 g • Carbohydrate 33 g • Fat 12 g • Fiber 1.3 g • Cholesterol 0 • Sodium 211 mg

TOFU CHOCOLATE FIG TARTS

I had dinner at Nobu Matsuhisa's famed restaurant in Los Angeles and ordered their chocolate fig tart. It was so delicious, I immediately went home and replicated it using tofu. This is the soy knockoff, but it sure tastes like the real thing.

MAKES 6 TARTS

6 individual 3-inch soy graham cracker tart shells (page 54)

12 ounces regular tofu

½ cup sugar or light granulated cane juice

¼ cup unsweetened cocoa powder

8 fresh Calimyrna figs, sliced thinly

1. Prepare tart shells according to the recipe or use storebought crusts.

2. In a food processor, puree the tofu until smooth. Add the sugar and cocoa; continue to process until thoroughly combined.

3. Pour the mixture evenly into the individual tart shells and shingle the figs across the top of the tart. Chill for 1 hour and serve.

NUTRIENT ANALYSIS
Calories 292 • Protein 6.6 g • Carbohydrate 47 g • Fat 9 g • Fiber 3 g • Cholesterol 0 • Sodium 159 mg

TOFU KEY LIME TARTLETS

South Florida's pride and joy, Key lime desserts are hard to re-create anywhere else. I consulted with a Miami-based foodie, and after a few tries, we got the desired result. For the best flavor and consistency, send away for the authentic Key lime juice.

**6 individual 3-inch graham
cracker tart shells
(page 54)**
12 ounces firm tofu
⅓ cup powdered sugar
2 tablespoons Key lime juice
Zest of 1 large lime

1. Prepare the tart shells according to the recipe or use storebought crusts.

2. In a food processor, puree the tofu until smooth, about 3 minutes.

3. Add the powdered sugar and Key lime juice. Continue to puree until smooth.

4. Pour into the individual tart shells and garnish each one with lime zest.

INGREDIENT TIP

Key lime juice is a specialty item that is not always easy to find. If you can't find it in your local market, call Florribian Key Lime Juice, 800-282-8459.

NUTRIENT ANALYSIS

Calories 184 • Protein 5.5 g • Carbohydrate 22 g • Fat 8.5 g • Fiber 1 g • Cholesterol 0 • Sodium 155 mg

TOFU LEMON TARTLETS

These lemon tartlets look like they're filled with authentic lemon curd, and their appearance fooled everyone at a birthday party I threw for my brother. The crust has a crunchy soynut flavor, and the custard filling is light and refreshing.

MAKES 6 TARTLETS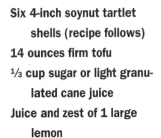

Six 4-inch soynut tartlet
    shells (recipe follows)
14 ounces firm tofu
1/3 cup sugar or light granu-
    lated cane juice
Juice and zest of 1 large
    lemon

1. Prepare the tartlet shells and set aside.

2. In a blender or food processor on medium speed, puree the tofu until smooth. Add the sugar and continue blending until thoroughly combined. Scrape down the sides of the blender if necessary.

3. Turn the blender or food processor on high and add the lemon juice and zest. Blend for 20 seconds.

4. Chill the lemon filling for 2 hours, then pour the mixture into the prepared tartlet shells and serve immediately.

NUTRIENT ANALYSIS
Calories 353 • Protein 16 g • Carbohydrate 39 g • Fat 15 g • Fiber 5.7 g • Cholesterol 0 • Sodium 15 mg

SOYNUT TARTLET CRUST

The toothsome crunch of the soynuts makes this tart crust a sturdy base for an endless variety of fillings. The dough yields enough for an 8-inch whole tart shell or 6 individual tartlets.

Six 4-inch tartlet pans or forms, nonstick preferred, with removable bottoms

1½ cups whole wheat pastry flour

1 cup roasted soynuts, finely chopped

3 tablespoons sugar or light granulated cane juice

⅓ cup soft soy margarine

⅓ cup ice-cold water

1. Preheat the oven to 350°F. Lightly grease each tartlet pan if not using nonstick.

2. In a large mixing bowl, combine the flour, soynuts, and sugar.

3. Add the margarine to the flour mixture. Using your fingers, work the ingredients together quickly until the mixture resembles coarse flakes.

4. Add the cold water gradually and mix with a spatula until the dough reaches a lumpy consistency and holds together. Be careful not to overmix or the crust will be tough. Gather it into a ball, cover with plastic, and refrigerate for at least 15 minutes.

5. Divide the dough into 6 equal parts and press it evenly into each tartlet pan. Make sure to cover all exposed areas of the pan.

6. Bake for 20 minutes, or until the shells turn brown. Cool completely and remove the tart shells from the pans before filling.

Dough can be made ahead and refrigerated for up to 1 week or frozen for up to 3 months.

NUTRIENT ANALYSIS

Calories 263 • Protein 10 g • Carbohydrate 27 g • Fat 13 g • Fiber 5.3 g • Cholesterol 0 • Sodium 9.7 mg

ITALIAN "TOFU RICOTTA" TART

Extra-firm tofu, when crumbled, will yield the consistency of ricotta cheese in this tofu version of the classic Italian ricotta tart. Raisins and apricots are cooked plump in orange juice, and the filling is then studded with pinenuts. The crust has a graham cracker cookie base for just the right crumble.

MAKES 10 SLICES

One 9-inch springform
    Graham Cracker Crust
    (page 54)
⅓ cup golden raisins
⅓ cup dried apricots,
    chopped (about 7 halves)
⅓ cup orange juice
1 pound extra-firm tofu
¾ cup sugar or light granu-
    lated cane juice
8 ounces soy cream cheese
¼ cup plain soy yogurt
Juice and zest of 1 lemon
2 tablespoons pine nuts

1. Prepare the Graham Cracker Crust ahead and set aside. Preheat the oven to 350°F.

2. In a small saucepan, heat the raisins and dried apricots in the orange juice, over very low heat, for about 5 minutes and set aside.

3. In a blender or food processor, puree the tofu until smooth. Add the sugar, soy cream cheese, soy yogurt, and lemon juice and zest, processing until smooth. Stir in the plumped fruit.

4. Pour the tofu mixture into the prepared piecrust and top with the pine nuts.

5. Bake for 50 minutes. Turn the oven off, leaving the tart in the oven for 1 hour. Remove and cool to room temperature. Refrigerate overnight before serving.

NUTRIENT ANALYSIS
Calories 277 • Protein 6.5 g • Carbohydrate 31 g • Fat 14 g • Fiber 1.4 g • Cholesterol 0 • Sodium 140 mg

QUICKBREADS, MUFFINS, BROWNIES, BARS, AND SCONES

If you are like most of us these days, always in a hurry, these are the recipes for you. All of the desserts in this chapter are quick and easy to prepare. These types of baked goods have an understated elegance and mystery to them. When you see how easy it is to put these together, they will become a staple in your personal entertaining repertoire.

Muffins, brownies, gingerbread, and scones are all well-known classics that most of us cannot resist. All of the recipes are great for brunch, a snack, a quick pick-me-up, or a treat to soothe you along with a cup of tea or coffee in the afternoon. Whether you like them homemade or storebought, the traditional versions of these recipes are generally made with eggs and cream, which results in great-tasting yet high-cholesterol items. Using soy yogurt or soy sour cream, the Soy Chocolate Chip Coffee Ring is indistinguishable from the traditional sour cream version. The Soy Lemon Pound Cake, the Soy Gingerbread, and the Soy Orange Spice Squares will make you reminisce about special holidays, and the soy flour and soy milk only serve to make them tastier. The Chocolate Soy Hearts with Cashew Soy Cream Frosting serve as a heart-healthy lover's treat, and the Soy Chocolate Raspberry Brownies are to live for! All the frostings on the cupcakes are interchangeable for a variety of flavor combinations, especially when entertaining. Both the Apricot Soy Scones and the Orange Soy Chocolate Chip Scones seem so fancy; yet they are a cinch to make and can be served at any time of day.

Fudgy Chocolate Soy Bundt Cake with Tofu Chocolate Mocha and Tofu Vanilla Drizzles

Soy Cream Tiramisù

Tofu Key Lime Tartlet

Tofu Lemon Tartlet

Tofu Custard Pie with Cherry Kiwi Topping

Soy Chocolate Raspberry Brownies

Soynut Brittle

Tofu Rocky Road Bars

Tofu S'mores

Orange Soy Chocolate Chip Scones

Soy Tollhouse Cookies

Oatmeal Raisin Soynut Cookies

Tofu Berry Trifle

Lemon Ginger Soy Ice Cream
with Lemon Soy Biscotti

Tofu Chocolate
Almond Mousse

Tofu Strawberry
Mousse

Tofu Pumpkin
Mousse

Assorted Soy Chocolate Truffles

Lemon Ginger Soy Ice Cream with Lemon Soy Biscotti

SOY CHOCOLATE CHIP COFFEE RING

Everyone I know has a favorite homemade quickbread that was always on the table when you went to visit Grandmother. Usually in the afternoon, the adults had it with coffee while the kids had it with cold milk. Mother could never quite replicate it, which made it extra special to visit. This version was adapted from a good friend's family recipe. She and her mother couldn't believe I replaced the sour cream with soy yogurt and got such great results!

MAKES 10 PIECES

¾ cup whole wheat pastry flour

¾ cup soy flour

1 teaspoon baking powder

½ teaspoon baking soda

½ cup sugar or light granulated cane juice

2 whole eggs

½ cup soy milk

6 ounces plain soy yogurt

FILLING/TOPPING

2 tablespoons sugar or light granulated cane juice

¼ teaspoon ground cinnamon

3 ounces semisweet soy chocolate chips

1. Preheat the oven to 350°F and lightly grease a 6-cup 8-inch bundt pan.

2. In a mixing bowl, combine the whole wheat pastry flour, soy flour, baking powder, and baking soda and mix well. In a separate bowl, combine the filling/topping ingredients and set aside.

3. In a blender or food processor, cream the sugar and eggs until fully combined. Add the soy milk and soy yogurt and continue to blend.

4. Add the soy milk mixture to the flour mixture and mix with a wire whisk.

5. Sprinkle 2 tablespoons cinnamon sugar and chocolate chips on the bottom of the greased bundt pan.

6. Place half of the batter in the pan and top with the filling mixture. Pour in the rest of the batter and bake for 55 minutes.

COOKING NOTES

This batter is very thick. Avoid the temptation to add more liquid to it. Just spoon the batter in with a rubber spatula and spread evenly. This coffee ring will rise beautifully!

Cinnamon sugar is a great topping for unfrosted cakes because it adds a little extra zing! Use equal portions of ground cinnamon to sugar or light granulated cane juice. If you have any cinnamon sugar left over, store it in a plastic airtight bag for future use.

NUTRIENT ANALYSIS

Calories 203 • Protein 6 g • Carbohydrate 37 g • Fat 4.5 g • Fiber 2.4 g • Cholesterol 42 mg • Sodium 132 mg

SOY CARROT RECTANGLES WITH SOY CREAM CHEESE FROSTING

There is a recipe for carrot cake with cream cheese frosting in every healthy-dessert cookbook ever printed! By cutting this soy version into rectangles, I gave it a look and taste that make an old-fashioned recipe new and exciting again.

MAKES 10 RECTANGLES

COOKING NOTE

For a lower-fat version, just sprinkle ¼ cup powdered sugar on top.

½ cup whole wheat pastry flour

¼ cup soy flour

1 teaspoon baking powder

¼ teaspoon cinnamon

1 whole egg

½ cup sugar or light granulated cane juice

¼ cup soybean oil

½ cup soy milk

1 teaspoon vanilla extract

1 cup grated carrots (2 carrots)

¼ cup finely chopped walnuts

½ cup Soy Cream Cheese Frosting (recipe follows)

½ cup shredded carrots, for garnish

1. Preheat the oven to 350°F. Lightly grease an 8 x 8-inch square baking pan.

2. In a large bowl, combine the whole wheat pastry flour, soy flour, baking powder, and cinnamon. Mix well.

3. In an electric mixer, cream the egg and sugar. Add the soybean oil, soy milk, and vanilla and mix thoroughly.

4. Add the flour mixture and beat until thoroughly combined. Fold in the grated carrots and walnuts.

5. Pour the batter into the greased pan. Bake for 35 minutes. Cool the cake to room temperature before frosting.

6. Remove the cake from the pan and frost with the Soy Cream Cheese Frosting. Cut into 10 rectangles and garnish with the shredded carrots.

Soy Carrot Rectangles will keep at room temperature in an airtight container for 3 days.

NUTRIENT ANALYSIS

Calories 164 • Protein 4.7 g • Carbohydrate 18 g • Fat 8.6 g • Fiber 1.8 g • Cholesterol 21 mg • Sodium 54 mg

Soy Cream Cheese Frosting

MAKES ½ CUP

4 ounces soy cream cheese

1 tablespoon soft soy margarine

½ cup powdered sugar

½ teaspoon vanilla extract

1. In a food processor, combine the soy cream cheese and margarine, puree until smooth, add the powdered sugar, and continue to process.

2. Add the vanilla and continue to mix until combined.

3. Refrigerate in an airtight container until ready to use.

NUTRIENT ANALYSIS

Calories 52 · Protein 0 · Carbohydrate 5.5 g · Fat 3.2 g · Fiber 0 · Cholesterol 0 · Sodium 54 mg

SOY GINGERBREAD

Gingerbread has a distinctive taste that always brings me back to the cold weather and winter holidays. This gingerbread recipe is light, easy to prepare, and can be enjoyed all year long. For a little extra flair, frost the gingerbread with Soy Cream Cheese Frosting (page 89).

MAKES 10 PIECES

½ cup whole wheat pastry flour

¼ cup soy flour

½ teaspoon baking soda

1 teaspoon ground ginger

½ teaspoon ground cinnamon

¼ teaspoon salt

¼ cup sugar or light granulated cane juice

2 tablespoons soft soy margarine

2 tablespoons molasses

2 tablespoons honey

¼ cup soy milk

1. Preheat the oven to 350°F. Lightly grease an 8 x 8-inch square baking pan.

2. In a mixing bowl, combine the whole wheat pastry flour, soy flour, baking soda, ginger, cinnamon, and salt.

3. In an electric mixer, cream the sugar and margarine until smooth.

4. Continue to beat and add the molasses, honey, and soy milk, one at a time.

5. Add the flour mixture and beat until thoroughly combined.

6. Pour into the prepared pan and bake for 1 hour. Cool completely and cut into squares, rectangles, or wedges.

NUTRIENT ANALYSIS

Calories 84 • Protein 2 g • Carbohydrate 14 g • Fat 2.6 g • Fiber 1.1 g • Cholesterol 0 • Sodium 124 mg

SOY LEMON POUND CAKE

The name "pound cake" comes from the original recipe in which each ingredient weighs a pound. Reminiscent of a traditional dense lemon pound cake, this lightened-up translation works great for a breakfast treat as well as a casual dessert. For a dressier version, serve with a drizzle of Soy Chocolate Sauce (page 153) and fresh berries.

MAKES 10 SLICES

½ cup whole wheat pastry flour

½ cup soy flour

½ teaspoon baking powder

¼ teaspoon baking soda

½ cup sugar or light granulated cane juice

⅓ cup soft soy margarine

2 egg whites

1¼ teaspoons lemon extract

½ cup soy milk

1 tablespoon lemon zest

TOPPING

½ cup powdered sugar

Juice of 1 lemon

1. Preheat the oven to 350°F and grease an 8 x 4½ x 2½-inch loaf pan.

2. In a separate bowl, combine the whole wheat pastry flour, soy flour, baking powder, and baking soda.

3. In an electric mixer or food processor, cream the sugar and margarine until smooth.

4. Add the egg whites and continue to mix; add the lemon extract and mix until combined.

5. Add the flour mixture to the creamed mixture gradually, alternating with the soy milk. Fold in the lemon zest.

6. Pour the batter into the prepared pan and bake for 1 hour. Let cool before removing.

7. Beat together the powdered sugar and lemon juice, and brush over the warm cake. Serve immediately.

This cake will keep, wrapped tightly, for 2 days.

NUTRIENT ANALYSIS

Calories 151 · Protein 3.9 g · Carbohydrate 21 g · Fat 6 g · Fiber 1.4 g · Cholesterol 0 · Sodium 65 mg

SOY PUMPKIN NUT LOAF

Looking for something unusual for the fall and winter holidays? This recipe is perfect for a holiday Thanksgiving buffet. This rich, flavorful Soy Pumpkin Nut Loaf combines great taste with the benefits of soy and healthy doses of antioxidants, beta-carotene, and vitamin E.

MAKES 10 SLICES

½ cup whole wheat pastry flour

¼ cup soy flour

½ teaspoon ground cinnamon

¼ teaspoon ground ginger

½ teaspoon ground nutmeg

3 whole eggs

1 cup sugar or light granulated cane juice

¾ cup pumpkin puree

½ cup chopped walnuts, toasted

1. Preheat the oven to 375°F. Lightly grease an 8½ x 2½-inch loaf pan.

2. In a mixing bowl, combine the whole wheat pastry flour, soy flour, cinnamon, ginger, and nutmeg.

3. In an electric mixer, cream the eggs and sugar until smooth. Add the pumpkin puree and continue to beat.

4. Gradually add the flour mixture to the egg mixture until thoroughly combined. Fold in the chopped walnuts.

5. Pour the batter into the prepared pan and bake for 1 hour. Cool completely before removing.

This loaf will keep, wrapped in plastic, for 3 days.

NUTRIENT ANALYSIS

Calories 106 • Protein 3.4 g • Carbohydrate 16 g • Fat 3.3 g • Fiber 1.1 g • Cholesterol 39 mg • Sodium 13 mg

BANANA SOY CHOCOLATE CHIP WALNUT SQUARES

My husband loves bananas, and so I always have a big bunch in my kitchen. When they start to sweeten, I look for new, creative ways to use them up. Banana and chocolate are a great combination. When you bake these squares, serve them with a dollop of Banana Chocolate Chip Soy Ice Cream (page 151).

 **MAKES 16 SQUARES**

1 cup whole wheat pastry
   flour
1 cup soy flour
2 teaspoons baking powder
½ teaspoon salt
½ cup sugar or light granulated cane juice
2 very ripe bananas, mashed
½ cup soybean oil
½ cup soy milk
¼ cup semisweet soy chocolate chips
¼ cup chopped walnuts

1. Preheat the oven to 350°F and grease an 8 x 8-inch square pan or line the pan with parchment paper.

2. In a large bowl, combine the whole wheat pastry flour, soy flour, baking powder, salt, and sugar.

3. In a separate bowl, combine the bananas, soybean oil, and soy milk and mix thoroughly.

4. Add the banana mixture to the dry mixture and stir until combined. Fold in the chocolate chips.

5. Pour the batter into the greased pan and sprinkle the walnuts on top. Bake for 40 minutes, or until an inserted toothpick comes out clean. Cool the cake to room temperature before slicing.

NUTRIENT ANALYSIS

Calories 175 · Protein 3 g · Carbohydrate 22 g · Fat 9 g · Fiber 2.6 g · Cholesterol 0 · Sodium 120 mg

SOY ORANGE SPICE SQUARES

That familiar scent of clove-spiked oranges that comes from homemade air fresheners is the inspiration for these spicy sweet squares made with soy. The combination tastes great and the kitchen aroma is wonderful!

MAKES 16 SQUARES

1 medium orange, peeled and sliced

2 tablespoons chopped walnuts

1 cup whole wheat pastry flour

1 cup soy flour

2 teaspoons baking powder

½ teaspoon baking soda

1 teaspoon ground cloves

¾ cup sugar or light granulated cane juice

1 cup soy milk

½ cup plain soy yogurt

¼ cup apple juice

1 tablespoon soybean oil

1. Preheat the oven to 350°F. Lightly grease an 8 x 8-inch square baking pan.

2. Zest the orange and cut off the remaining peel. Thinly slice the orange into 6 slices and line the bottom of the pan with them. Sprinkle the walnuts over the oranges and set aside.

3. In a large bowl, combine the whole wheat pastry flour, soy flour, baking powder, baking soda, cloves, and sugar.

4. In a separate bowl, combine the soy milk, soy yogurt, apple juice, and soybean oil.

5. Add the soy milk mixture to the flour mixture, and beat until thoroughly combined.

6. Pour the batter into the prepared pan and bake for 35 minutes, or until an inserted toothpick comes out clean. Cool the cake to room temperature before slicing.

NUTRIENT ANALYSIS

Calories 114 • Protein 4.6 g • Carbohydrate 20 g • Fat 2 g • Fiber 2.2 g • Cholesterol 39 mg • Sodium 96 mg

CHOCOLATE SOY HEARTS WITH CASHEW SOY CREAM FROSTING

These beautiful heart-shaped delicacies are perfect for a Valentine's Day surprise. Serve them as a healthy love potion: not only will you benefit from the soy, but chocolate contains compounds that make you feel like you're in love, and that is really good for your heart.

 **MAKES 10 HEARTS**

1 cup whole wheat pastry
    flour
½ cup soy flour
1 tablespoon baking soda
1 cup sugar or light granu-
    lated cane juice
½ cup unsweetened cocoa
    powder
1½ cups whole soy milk
1 tablespoon soybean oil
1 teaspoon vanilla extract
One 3-inch heart-shaped
    cookie cutter
¾ cup Cashew Soy Cream
    Frosting (recipe follows)
½ cup cashews, for garnish

1. Preheat the oven to 350°F and grease two 8-inch square cake pans. Line a cookie sheet with parchment paper.

2. In a large bowl, combine the whole wheat pastry flour, soy flour, baking soda, sugar, and cocoa. Mix well and set aside.

3. In a separate bowl, combine the soy milk, soybean oil, and vanilla. Pour this mixture into the flour mixture, stirring with a wire whisk until well combined.

4. Pour the batter into the greased pans and bake for 25 minutes, or until the cakes spring back when touched. Cool completely.

5. Invert the cakes onto the cookie sheet. With the heart-shaped cookie cutter, cut out 10 cakes, 5 from each pan.

6. Frost each heart with the Cashew Soy Cream Frosting, and garnish each one with 3 whole cashews.

After frosting, these hearts will keep, wrapped, in the refrigerator for 2 days.

NUTRIENT ANALYSIS
Calories 291 · Protein 8.6 g · Carbohydrate 42 g · Fat 10 g · Fiber 3.5 g · Cholesterol 0 · Sodium 189 mg

Cashew Soy Cream Frosting

¼ cup cashews

4 ounces regular tofu

4 ounces soy cream cheese

3 tablespoons sugar or light
   granulated cane juice

1. In a food processor, chop the cashews to a finely ground consistency.

2. Add the tofu, soy cream cheese, and sugar and puree until smooth. Refrigerate until ready to use.

This frosting will keep, wrapped, for 5 days.

NUTRIENT ANALYSIS

Calories 72 • Protein 1.7 g • Carbohydrate 5.3 g • Fat 5.1 g • Fiber 0.2 g • Cholesterol 0 • Sodium 58 mg

CHOCOLATE DEVIL'S FOOD SOY CUPCAKES WITH CHOCOLATE SOY FROSTING

The term "devil's food" gives the impression of naughtiness to this recipe. With a healthful, guiltless twist, these cupcakes bring a smile to everyone's face. Adults and children alike will marvel at how these cupcakes are as satisfying as any bakeshop version.

MAKES 12
CUPCAKES

½ cup whole wheat pastry flour

½ cup soy flour

¼ cup unsweetened cocoa powder

½ teaspoon baking soda

¼ teaspoon salt

¾ cup sugar or light granulated cane juice

5 tablespoons soft soy margarine

1 teaspoon vanilla extract

2 large eggs

½ cup soy milk

¾ cup Chocolate Soy Frosting (recipe follows)

1. Preheat the oven to 350°F. Line a 12-count muffin pan with paper muffin liners.

2. In a mixing bowl, combine the whole wheat pastry flour, soy flour, cocoa, baking soda, and salt.

3. In an electric mixer, cream the sugar and margarine until smooth. Add the vanilla.

4. Add the eggs, one at a time, beating well.

5. Alternately add the flour mixture and the soy milk to the liquid. Beat until thoroughly combined.

6. Spoon the batter into the lined muffin tins. Bake for 20 minutes. Cool for 10 minutes before frosting. While the muffins are baking, prepare the frosting.

CHOCOLATE SOY FROSTING

MAKES ¾ CUP

¼ cup sugar or light granulated cane juice

1 tablespoon soft soy margarine

3 tablespoons soy milk

1 teaspoon vanilla extract

1 cup unsweetened cocoa powder

1¾ cups powdered sugar

1. In an electric mixer, cream the sugar and margarine until smooth.

2. Continue to beat and add the soy milk. Gradually beat in the vanilla, cocoa, and powdered sugar, beating just until combined. Frost the cooled cupcakes immediately.

These cupcakes will keep, wrapped in plastic, for 2 days.

NUTRIENT ANALYSIS

Calories 248 • Protein 5.8 g • Carbohydrate 39 g • Fat 7.8 g • Fiber 3.5 g • Cholesterol 35 mg • Sodium 120 mg

BANANA SOY CUPCAKES WITH SOY CREAM CHEESE WALNUT FROSTING

These are the quintessential "nutritious" muffins. Traditional and timeless, bananas and walnuts are a winning, healthful combination. With the addition of soy, it is even more rewarding!

MAKES 12
CUPCAKES

½ cup whole wheat pastry flour

½ cup soy flour

½ teaspoon baking soda

¼ teaspoon salt

¾ cup sugar or light granu-lated cane juice

¼ cup soy margarine

2 large very ripe bananas, mashed

1 teaspoon vanilla extract

2 whole eggs

¼ cup plain soy yogurt

¾ cup Soy Cream Cheese Walnut Frosting (recipe follows)

1. Line a 12-count muffin pan with paper muffin liners.

2. In a mixing bowl, combine the whole wheat pastry flour, soy flour, baking soda, and salt.

3. In an electric mixer, cream the sugar and margarine until smooth. Add the bananas and vanilla.

4. Add the eggs, one at a time, beating well.

5. Alternately add the flour mixture and the soy yogurt to the liquid. Beat until thoroughly combined.

6. Spoon the batter into the lined muffin tins. Bake for 20 minutes. Cool for 10 minutes before frosting. While the muffins are baking, prepare the frosting.

COOKING NOTE
This recipe is great when you have ripe bananas lying around ready to throw out.

Soy Cream Cheese Walnut Frosting

1¾ cups powdered sugar
½ cup (4 ounces) soy cream cheese
½ teaspoon vanilla extract
2 tablespoons chopped walnuts

1. In an electric mixer, cream the sugar and soy cream cheese until smooth.

2. Continue to beat and add the vanilla.

3. Fold in the walnuts and frost the cooled cupcakes immediately.

These cupcakes will keep, wrapped in plastic, for 2 days.

NUTRIENT ANALYSIS

Calories 237 • Protein 4.6 g • Carbohydrate 36 g • Fat 8.6 g • Fiber 1.6 g • Cholesterol 35 mg • Sodium 160 mg

SOYNUT BUTTER CUPCAKES WITH SOYNUT BUTTER FROSTING

Packed with nutrition from soy, and with a "stick to the roof of your mouth" quality, these cupcakes provide the same nutty taste and texture as the original peanut butter version. Decorate with the Soynut Butter Frosting, or just spread a little strawberry jam on top.

MAKES 12 CUPCAKES

¾ cup whole wheat pastry flour

½ cup soy flour

1¼ teaspoons baking powder

¼ teaspoon salt

½ cup sugar or light granulated cane juice

¼ cup soynut butter

3 tablespoons soft soy margarine

1 teaspoon vanilla extract

1 whole egg

¾ cup Soynut Butter Frosting (recipe follows)

1. Preheat the oven to 350°F. Line a 12-count muffin pan with paper muffin liners.

2. In a mixing bowl, combine the whole wheat pastry flour, soy flour, baking powder, and salt.

3. In an electric mixer, beat the sugar, soynut butter, margarine, and vanilla until smooth, about 5 minutes. Add the egg, beating well.

4. Alternately add the flour mixture and the soynut butter mixture to the liquid. Beat until thoroughly combined.

5. Spoon the batter into the lined muffin tins. Bake for 20 minutes. Cool for 10 minutes before frosting. While the muffins are baking, prepare the frosting.

Soynut Butter Frosting

MAKES ¾ CUP

1 tablespoon soft soy margarine

¼ cup sugar or light granulated cane juice

2 tablespoons soynut butter

¼ cup soy milk

1 teaspoon vanilla extract

1¾ cups powdered sugar

In a saucepan heat the margarine over medium heat. Add the sugar and the soynut butter, stirring constantly. Add the soy milk and stir until smooth. Remove from the heat and cool. Gradually beat in the vanilla and the powdered sugar, beating just until combined. Frost the cooled cupcakes immediately.

NUTRIENT ANALYSIS

Calories 201 • Protein 5 g • Carbohydrate 31 g • Fat 6.7 g • Fiber 1.7 g • Cholesterol 17 mg • Sodium 137 mg

MAPLE SOY CUPCAKES WITH MAPLE SYRUP FROSTING

I find these muffins to be the ultimate comfort snack because maple soy muffins evoke a homey, New England feeling. Serve them hot, right out of the oven, or cool them and frost for dessert.

MAKES 12 CUPCAKES

¾ cup whole wheat pastry flour

½ cup soy flour

1¼ teaspoons baking powder

¼ teaspoon salt

½ cup sugar or light granulated cane juice

5 tablespoons soft soy margarine

1 teaspoon vanilla extract

2 large eggs

¼ cup soy milk

¼ cup pure maple syrup

¾ cup Maple Syrup Frosting (recipe follows)

1. Preheat the oven to 350°F. Line a 12-count muffin pan with paper muffin liners.

2. In a mixing bowl, combine the whole wheat pastry flour, soy flour, baking powder, and salt.

3. In an electric mixer, cream the sugar and margarine until smooth. Add the vanilla.

4. Add the eggs, one at a time, beating well.

5. In another bowl, combine the soy milk and maple syrup.

6. Alternately add the flour mixture and the sugar-margarine mixture to the soymilk mixture. Beat until thoroughly combined.

7. Spoon the batter into the lined muffin tins. Bake for 20 minutes. Cool for 10 minutes before frosting. While the muffins are baking, prepare the frosting.

Maple Syrup Frosting

MAKES ¾ CUP

6 tablespoons pure maple syrup

2 tablespoons soft soy margarine

½ teaspoon vanilla extract

1¾ cups powdered sugar

1. In an electric mixer, beat the maple syrup, margarine, and vanilla until smooth.

2. Add the powdered sugar, beating just until blended.

3. Frost the cooled cupcakes.

NUTRIENT ANALYSIS

Calories 242 • Protein 3.9 g • Carbohydrate 40 g • Fat 7.9 g • Fiber 1.3 g • Cholesterol 35 mg • Sodium 106 mg

SOY CHOCOLATE RASPBERRY BROWNIES

These soy chocolate raspberry brownies are so chocolaty and satisfying, I call them the dessert to "live for." The fat and calories are so low, but they still have that luscious mouth feel that you expect from chocolate. Serve with Raspberry Sauce (page 58) for a little extra sweetness.

½ cup whole wheat pastry flour

½ cup soy flour

¼ teaspoon baking powder

2 whole eggs

1 cup sugar or light granulated cane juice

3 tablespoons soft soy margarine

⅓ cup semisweet soy chocolate chips

¼ cup raspberry jam

1. Preheat the oven to 350°F and lightly grease an 8-inch round or square cake pan.

2. In a mixing bowl, combine the whole wheat pastry flour, soy flour, and baking powder and set aside.

3. In an electric mixer, cream the eggs and sugar until smooth.

4. In a double boiler over medium heat, melt the margarine and chocolate chips, stir until smooth, and remove from the heat.

5. Add the chocolate mixture to the egg mixture a little at a time, and continue to beat.

6. Slowly incorporate the flour mixture into the liquid mixture. Beat slowly and gradually increase speed until well combined.

7. Fold in the jam and pour into the prepared cake pan.

8. Bake for 30 minutes. Let cool before removing.

Brownies can be stored in an airtight container for 3 days.

COOKING NOTE

These brownies can be cut into the traditional squares, or baked in a round pan and cut into decorative wedges.

NUTRIENT ANALYSIS

Calories 234 • Protein 4.7 g • Carbohydrate 37 g • Fat 9 g • Fiber 2 g • Cholesterol 42 mg • Sodium 71.5 mg

SOY CHOCOLATE PEPPERMINT BROWNIES

This version is just as rich as the Soy Chocolate Raspberry Brownies, yet the mint adds a refreshing coolness to the chocolate. These are great for a summer dessert and travel well in a picnic basket.

MAKES 10 BROWNIES

2 whole eggs

1 cup sugar or light granulated cane juice

½ cup whole wheat pastry flour

½ cup soy flour

¼ teaspoon baking powder

3 tablespoons soft soy margarine

⅓ cup semisweet soy chocolate chips

1 tablespoon peppermint extract

1. Preheat the oven to 350°F and lightly grease an 8-inch round cake pan.

2. In an electric mixer, cream the eggs and sugar until smooth.

3. In a mixing bowl, combine the whole wheat pastry flour, soy flour, and baking powder and set aside.

4. In a double boiler over medium heat, melt the margarine and chocolate chips, stir until smooth, and remove from the heat.

5. A little at a time, add the chocolate mixture to the egg mixture and continue to beat. Add the peppermint extract. Mix.

6. Add the flour mixture to the chocolate mixture. Beat slowly and gradually increase speed until well combined.

7. Pour the mixture into the prepared cake pan.

8. Bake for 30 minutes. Let cool before removing.

Brownies can be stored in an airtight container for 3 days.

NUTRIENT ANALYSIS

Calories 226 • Protein 4.7 g • Carbohydrate 34 g • Fat 9 g • Fiber 2 g • Cholesterol 42 mg • Sodium 73 mg

SOYNUT BUTTER CHOCOLATE BROWNIES

Chocolate and peanut butter are another tried-and-true American classic. Using soynut butter, I am giving Reese's Peanut Butter Cups a run for their money.

MAKES 10 BROWNIES

2 whole eggs

1 cup sugar or light granulated cane juice

½ cup whole wheat pastry flour

½ cup soy flour

¼ teaspoon baking powder

3 tablespoons soft soy margarine

⅓ cup semisweet soy chocolate chips (5 ounces)

¼ cup soynut butter

¼ cup roasted soynuts

1. Preheat the oven to 350°F and lightly grease an 8-inch round cake pan.

2. In an electric mixer, cream the eggs and sugar until smooth.

3. In a mixing bowl, combine the whole wheat pastry flour, soy flour, and baking powder and set aside.

4. In a double boiler over medium heat, melt the margarine and chocolate chips, stir until smooth, and remove from the heat.

5. A little at a time, add the chocolate mixture to the egg mixture and continue to beat. Add the soynut butter and thoroughly combine.

6. Add the flour mixture to the chocolate mixture. Beat slowly and gradually increase speed until well combined.

7. Fold in the soynuts, and pour into the prepared cake pan.

8. Bake for 30 minutes. Let cool before removing.

Brownies can be stored in an airtight container for 3 days.

NUTRIENT ANALYSIS

Calories 267 • Protein 7.2 g • Carbohydrate 37 g • Fat 11 g • Fiber 2.6 g • Cholesterol 42 mg • Sodium 109 mg

APRICOT SOY SCONES

A perfect balance of crumbly and moist, these scones are a great "soy healthy" snack. Served warm with jam, they always hit the spot. If apricots are not your thing, use a variety of different dried fruits in direct proportion. Be creative and have fun.

MAKES 12 SCONES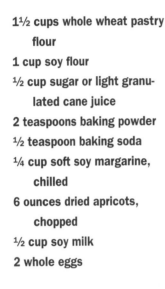

1½ cups whole wheat pastry flour

1 cup soy flour

½ cup sugar or light granulated cane juice

2 teaspoons baking powder

½ teaspoon baking soda

¼ cup soft soy margarine, chilled

6 ounces dried apricots, chopped

½ cup soy milk

2 whole eggs

1. Preheat the oven to 400°F. Lightly grease a cookie sheet and set aside.

2. In a mixing bowl, combine the whole wheat pastry flour, soy flour, sugar, baking powder, and baking soda.

3. Add the margarine and cut with a pastry cutter until the mixture resembles coarse crumbs. Stir in the apricots.

4. In a separate bowl, combine the soy milk and eggs, stirring vigorously. Add to the flour mixture and stir just until moistened.

5. Turn the dough out onto a lightly floured surface and knead until it is no longer sticky.

6. Form the dough into a flattened circle, about 3 inches thick, on the prepared cookie sheet. Cut the dough only halfway through into 12 wedge-shaped slices.

7. Bake for 20 minutes. Serve immediately while they are still warm.

NUTRIENT ANALYSIS

Calories 193 • Protein 7.3 g • Carbohydrate 30 g • Fat 5.6 g • Fiber 3.9 g • Cholesterol 35 mg • Sodium 129 mg

ORANGE SOY CHOCOLATE CHIP SCONES

Orange and chocolate give these scones a sweet, refreshing twist on a timeless treat. This recipe is so easy to prepare, and cuts the fat to less than half of that in the original butter version. Mix and match with lemon and raisins for another flavor combination.

 **MAKES 12 SCONES**

1½ cups whole wheat pastry flour

1 cup soy flour

½ cup sugar or light granulated cane juice

2 teaspoons baking powder

½ teaspoon baking soda

¼ cup soft soy margarine, chilled

½ cup semisweet soy chocolate chips

Zest of 1 orange

½ cup soy milk

2 large eggs

1. Preheat the oven to 400°F. Lightly grease a cookie sheet and set aside.

2. In a mixing bowl, combine the whole wheat pastry flour, soy flour, sugar, baking powder, and baking soda.

3. Add the margarine and cut with a pastry cutter until the mixture resembles coarse crumbs. Stir in the chocolate chips and orange zest.

4. In a separate bowl, combine the soy milk and eggs, stirring vigorously. Add to the flour mixture and stir just until moistened.

5. Turn the dough out onto a lightly floured surface and knead until it is no longer sticky.

6. Form the dough into a flattened circle, about 3 inches thick, on the prepared cookie sheet. Cut the dough only halfway through into 12 wedge-shaped slices.

7. Bake for 20 minutes. Serve immediately while they are still warm.

NUTRIENT ANALYSIS
Calories 193 • Protein 7.1 g • Carbohydrate 26 g • Fat 7.6 g • Fiber 3.1 g • Cholesterol 35 mg • Sodium 128 mg

CANDY AND COOKIES

These bite-sized treats are a joy to prepare because of the thrill that candy and cookies provide for everyone. Candies and cookies are universally accepted as a way to show love and gratitude and provide nourishment to all, and they make people of all ages happy. As a gift, bribe, and a token of affection, a sweet, little delicacy can get you very far. Holidays and special occasions always go hand in hand with these little jewels, and having healthier versions around will satisfy everyone's individual dietary requests.

Lately there has been so much talk of reducing the refined sugars in our diets, we can't help but hesitate and think of this every time we pass a bakeshop or chocolatier. The incredible ease of preparation, the organic light granulated cane juice, and the all-natural chocolate chips used in these recipes are a health food lover's dream to work with. Soynuts can replace other kinds of nuts or enhance a recipe, and tofu is a great substitute for marshmallows in the Tofu Rocky Road Bars and the Tofu S'mores. Eating and forming melted chocolate on its own is wonderful, but when mixed with other ingredients it takes on a complexity of flavors that is hard to resist.

Candy making is an art and science that is taken very seriously. Candy is not necessarily unhealthy, and when soy-based, organic ingredients are used, the subtle benefits will outweigh the health concerns that people have today about eating sweets. By closely following the procedures in this chapter, you can become a master candy maker of such elegant recipes as Coconut Soy Chocolate Truffles or Soynut Brittle. The casual Soynut Carrot Chocolate Haystacks are perfect for a picnic or Sunday brunch. They are great-tasting, healthy, and really easy to prepare.

The word "cookie" actually means a small cake. There are thousands of cookie recipes in the world, and you can use soy products in all of them. Soy flour, soy milk, tofu, soynuts, and soy chocolate chips are all included in this chapter. New interpretations of some well-known, basic cookie recipes are here: Soy Tollhouse Cookies, Oatmeal Raisin Soynut Cookies, Soynut Balls, and Almond Soy Drop Cookies. I include the Cardamom Anise Tofu Squares and the Lemon Soy Biscotti to appeal to those with more esoteric inclinations.

TOFU ROCKY ROAD BARS

Snowy bits of marshmallow are what make up the "rocks" in Rocky Road. I use an extra-firm tofu and roasted soynuts to replicate the rugged texture of this universally loved candy.

½ cup roasted soynuts

4 ounces extra-firm tofu, drained and diced

1 cup semisweet soy chocolate chips

⅓ cup soy milk

1. Lightly grease an 8 x 5-inch rectangular pan and spread the soynuts and the diced tofu evenly across the bottom.

2. Put the chocolate chips in a glass bowl.

3. In a small saucepan, heat the soy milk over a medium-high flame just until it starts to boil.

4. Remove from the heat and pour directly over the chocolate chips and whisk quickly until smooth. Watch carefully, as this mixture has a tendency to form lumps.

5. Immediately pour the chocolate mixture slowly and evenly over the nuts and tofu. Gently spread to cover the whole pan.

6. Cover with plastic wrap and refrigerate for at least 2 hours.

COOKING NOTE

For extra-firm tofu, put the tofu, uncut, into a colander and let sit for 1 hour. This will drain out any excess water that might cause the end product to be mushy.

NUTRIENT ANALYSIS

Calories 57 • Protein 1.2 g • Carbohydrate 7 g • Fat 3.4 g • Fiber 0.8 g • Cholesterol 0 • Sodium 2.3 mg

SOYNUT BRITTLE

Soynut brittle is always a big hit with my family and friends. Very simply, I replaced peanuts with soynuts. It is a joy to prepare, especially because of the wonderful aroma of the nuts in the molten sugar while it is cooking.

MAKES 1 POUND, OR 16 PIECES

2 cups sugar or light granulated cane juice

1½ cups roasted soynuts

COOKING NOTE

It is important to work fast when pouring the mixture onto the aluminum foil. When you remove the melted nut mixture from the heat, it starts to solidify immediately.

1. Line a cookie sheet with aluminum foil.

2. In a small saucepan, over high heat, bring the sugar to a boil, stirring constantly with a metal wire whisk to avoid lumps.

3. Add the soynuts and cook for one more minute.

4. Pour the mixture onto the prepared cookie sheet, spreading evenly, about ½ inch thick.

5. Let cool, about 30 minutes, and peel off the aluminum foil. Break into small pieces to serve.

These will store well in a sealed container at room temperature for 2 weeks.

VARIATION
Substitute ½ cup of any other nut for flavor variety.

NUTRIENT ANALYSIS
Calories 127 • Protein 3.1 g • Carbohydrate 25 g • Fat 1.5 g • Fiber 0.8 g • Cholesterol 0 • Sodium 2.4 mg

ASSORTED SOY CHOCOLATE TRUFFLES

Smooth and creamy, truffles are the most elegant and easiest of all candies to make. I use whole soy milk instead of cream, which requires a higher proportion of chocolate. Roll them in chopped soynuts, shredded coconut, or cocoa powder for a truly memorable experience.

2½ cups semisweet soy
    chocolate chips
    (1 pound)
¾ cup soy milk
Cornstarch, for dusting

COATINGS
½ cup soynuts, ground
½ cup shredded coconut
½ cup unsweetened cocoa
    powder

1. Put the chocolate chips in a large glass bowl and set aside.

2. In a small saucepan, heat the soy milk over a high flame just until it starts to boil.

3. Remove the milk from the heat and pour directly over the chocolate chips; whisk vigorously until smooth.

4. Pour into a plastic container, cover, and place in the refrigerator for 1 hour.

5. Place the three different coatings on individual plates or in shallow bowls.

6. Use a melon baller or a miniature ice cream scoop dusted with cornstarch to scoop the chocolate mixture into balls. Roll the balls in ground soynuts, shredded coconut, or cocoa powder to cover completely. Place in paper candy cups or on a doily and serve immediately. To store, freeze the mixture in an airtight container for up to 1 month before forming the balls.

NUTRIENT ANALYSIS — SOYNUT

Calories 72 • Protein 1.1 g • Carbohydrate 8.9 g • Fat 4.4 g • Fiber 0.9 g • Cholesterol 0 • Sodium 5 mg

NUTRIENT ANALYSIS — COCONUT

Calories 71 • Protein 0.7 g • Carbohydrate 8.8 g • Fat 4.5 g • Fiber 0.9 g • Cholesterol 0 • Sodium 2.4 mg

NUTRIENT ANALYSIS — COCOA POWDER

Calories 83 • Protein 1.2 g • Carbohydrate 12 g • Fat 4.3 g • Fiber 0.9 g • Cholesterol 0 • Sodium 25 mg

SOYNUT CARROT CHOCOLATE HAYSTACKS

My father gobbles up candy when he sees it, and asks, "What's in these?" afterward. With this easy quick recipe, I can rest assured that he will finally enjoy something that is good for him.

MAKES 12 CLUSTERS

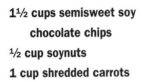

1½ cups semisweet soy
chocolate chips

½ cup soynuts

1 cup shredded carrots

1. Line a cookie sheet with parchment paper and set aside.

2. In a small saucepan, over medium heat, melt the chocolate chips, whisking constantly until smooth.

3. Add the soynuts and carrots, quickly toss in the melted chocolate, and spoon out 12 portions onto the prepared cookie sheet. Cool completely and serve.

These can be stored in a plastic container for 5 days.

NUTRIENT ANALYSIS
Calories 139 • Protein 3 g • Carbohydrate 17 g • Fat 8 g • Fiber 2.1 g • Cholesterol 0 • Sodium 7.2 mg

CARDAMOM ANISE TOFU SQUARES

Cardamom and anise are a classic combination in Indian cooking. Try these after a hot spicy meal, for good digestion.

10 ounces extra-firm tofu

½ cup sugar or light granulated cane juice

1 teaspoon ground cardamom

2 teaspoons anise extract or anisette liqueur

1. Preheat the oven to 350°F.

2. Drain the water from the tofu and cut into 6 slices the long way and then across to form 12 squares.

3. Place the tofu slices on an ungreased cookie sheet and bake for 20 minutes.

4. Remove the tofu from the oven and transfer to another cookie sheet or glass baking dish. Set the pieces far apart for coating. Cool completely.

5. In a small saucepan, on high heat, bring the sugar to a boil, stirring constantly with a metal wire whisk to avoid lumps.

6. Add the cardamom and anise and cook for 30 more seconds.

7. Remove from the heat and coat each piece of tofu with the sugar mixture. Let cool and harden. Serve immediately.

NUTRIENT ANALYSIS
Calories 89 • Protein 2.4 g • Carbohydrate 16 g • Fat 1.2 g • Fiber 0 • Cholesterol 0 • Sodium 2.5 mg

TOFU CHOCOLATE MINT BARS

These are the soy version of Andes Candies. Chocolate, mint, and creamy tofu give this bar just the right combination of flavor and texture for a refreshing after-dinner treat.

MAKES 12 BARS

SIZE NOTE
The 8½ x 5½ x 1-inch pan is a standard disposable pan you can find in the supermarket.

CRUST

3 tablespoons soft soy margarine

½ cup graham cracker crumbs

FILLING

6 ounces soft tofu

¼ cup sugar or light granulated cane juice

2 ounces soy cream cheese

1 teaspoon mint extract

TOPPING

½ cup Soy Chocolate Ganache (page 39)

1. Preheat the oven to 350°F. In a mixing bowl, combine the margarine and graham cracker crumbs and press the mixture into a disposable pan (see Size Note).

2. In a blender or food processor, puree the tofu until smooth. Add the sugar, soy cream cheese, and mint extract, processing until smooth. Scrape down the sides as necessary.

3. Pour the tofu mixture into the prepared piecrust and bake for 30 minutes. Remove from the oven and cool for 1 hour.

4. Prepare the Soy Chocolate Ganache and top immediately.

Refrigerate for 4 hours or overnight.

NUTRIENT ANALYSIS
Calories 135 • Protein 2.4 g • Carbohydrate 14 g • Fat 8 g • Fiber 0.6 g • Cholesterol 0 • Sodium 98 mg

TOFU CHOCOLATE MARBLE BARS

Any desserts that have intricate patterns in them always get "ohs" and "ahs." When you add the chocolate mixture to the cream cheese mixture, swirl it around to make your own personal design.

CRUST
3 tablespoons soft soy margarine
½ cup graham cracker crumbs

FILLING
6 ounces soft tofu
¼ cup sugar or light granulated cane juice
2 ounces soy cream cheese
1 teaspoon almond extract
1 tablespoon unsweetened cocoa powder

TOPPING
½ cup Soy Chocolate Ganache (page 39)

1. Preheat the oven to 350°F. In a mixing bowl, combine the margarine and graham cracker crumbs and press the mixture into an 8½ x 5½ x 1-inch disposable pan.

2. In a blender or food processor, puree the tofu until smooth. Add the sugar, soy cream cheese, and almond extract, processing until smooth. Scrape down the sides as necessary.

3. Transfer half of the tofu mixture into another bowl and set aside.

4. Add the cocoa to the remaining half of the tofu mixture, process until thoroughly mixed. Pour the plain tofu mixture into the prepared piecrust, and then with a spoon, blend in the chocolate tofu mixture in a marbleized pattern.

5. Bake for 30 minutes. Remove from the oven and cool for 1 hour.

6. Prepare the Soy Chocolate Ganache and top immediately. Refrigerate for 4 hours or overnight.

> **ENTERTAINING TIP**
> When entertaining, make one double batch of tofu cream cheese filling and piecrust. Divide into four portions and flavor the bars individually and bake them all together.

NUTRIENT ANALYSIS
Calories 137 • Protein 2.6 g • Carbohydrate 13 g • Fat 8 g • Fiber 0.8 g • Cholesterol 0 • Sodium 98 mg

SOY TOLLHOUSE COOKIES

Serve fresh out of the oven with a glass of soy milk . . . need I say more?

MAKES 24 COOKIES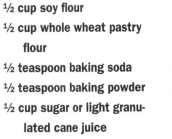

½ cup soy flour

½ cup whole wheat pastry
flour

½ teaspoon baking soda

½ teaspoon baking powder

½ cup sugar or light granulated cane juice

⅓ cup soft soy margarine

⅓ cup soy milk

1 teaspoon vanilla extract

⅓ cup soy espresso choco-
late chips

1. Preheat the oven to 350°F and line two cookie sheets with parchment paper.

2. In a mixing bowl, combine the soy flour, whole wheat pastry flour, baking soda, and baking powder.

3. In an electric mixer, cream the sugar and margarine until smooth; add the soy milk and vanilla. Add to the flour mixture and mix until the dough is stiff.

4. Fold in the chocolate chips and roll the dough out onto a floured surface. Form into two logs and cut them into ½-inch slices. Place the slices evenly onto the lined cookie sheets.

5. Bake for 12 to 15 minutes, or until slightly browned.

NUTRIENT ANALYSIS
Calories 72 • Protein 1.4 g • Carbohydrate 9.2 g • Fat 4 g • Fiber 0.7 g • Cholesterol 0 • Sodium 35 mg

OATMEAL RAISIN SOYNUT COOKIES

These cookies, whether the original version or soy-based, are an ever-popular choice for children and adults alike. They are great for packing in lunch bags and picnics, but they usually don't last long enough to have leftovers.

 **MAKES 24 COOKIES**

½ cup whole wheat pastry
    flour

½ cup soy flour

⅛ teaspoon salt

1 cup old-fashioned rolled
    oats

½ cup sugar or light granu-
    lated cane juice

½ cup brown sugar or dark
    granulated cane juice

⅓ cup soft soy margarine

½ cup soy milk

1 teaspoon vanilla extract

¼ cup raisins

¼ cup soynuts

1. Preheat the oven to 350°F and line two cookie sheets with parchment paper.

2. In a mixing bowl, combine the whole wheat pastry flour, soy flour, salt, and rolled oats.

3. In an electric mixer, cream the sugars and margarine until smooth; add the soy milk and vanilla.

4. Add the flour mixture to the creamed sugar mixture and mix until thoroughly combined.

5. Fold in the raisins and soynuts and spoon out heaping tablespoons of dough on the lined cookie sheets. Slightly flatten the top of each cookie. Bake for 20 minutes, or until slightly browned.

NUTRIENT ANALYSIS

Calories 100 • Protein 2.2 g • Carbohydrate 13 g • Fat 4.5 g • Fiber 1 g • Cholesterol 0 • Sodium 68 mg

SOYNUT BALLS

These are reminiscent of Mexican wedding cookies. Just a few slight changes turn them into rich and nutty festive nuggets.

MAKES 12 BALLS

1 cup soynuts (3 ounces), finely chopped

½ cup whole wheat pastry flour

½ cup soy flour

⅓ cup light granulated cane juice

½ cup soft soy margarine

1 teaspoon vanilla extract

1 cup powdered sugar

1. Preheat the oven to 350°F. Line a cookie sheet with parchment paper and set aside.

2. Combine the soynuts, whole wheat pastry flour, soy flour, and light granulated cane juice.

3. Add the margarine and vanilla and mix thoroughly.

4. By hand, form the dough into 12 balls and place evenly on the cookie sheet.

5. Bake for 15 minutes and cool completely.

6. Roll each ball in the powdered sugar and serve.

Store in an airtight container for 2 days.

NUTRIENT ANALYSIS
Calories 149 • Protein 5.2 g • Carbohydrate 12 g • Fat 9 g • Fiber 1.6 g • Cholesterol 0 • Sodium 5.5 mg

ALMOND SOY DROP COOKIES

Soft and chewy, these drop cookies are laced with minced almonds and would go well with a glass of amaretto. Perfect for a evening by the fire.

1 cup almonds (3 ounces), finely chopped

1 cup whole wheat pastry flour

1 cup soy flour

1/3 cup sugar or light granulated cane juice

1/2 cup soft soy margarine

1/4 cup soy yogurt

2 tablespoons soy milk

1. Preheat the oven to 350°F. Line a cookie sheet with parchment paper and set aside.

2. Combine the almonds, whole wheat pastry flour, soy flour, and sugar.

3. Add the margarine and mix thoroughly to form the consistency of coarse crumbs.

4. Add the soy yogurt and soy milk to form a soft, sticky dough.

5. Form the dough into 16 portions with a heaping tablespoon and place evenly on the cookie sheet.

6. Bake for 20 minutes and cool completely.

7. Serve immediately or store in an airtight container for 4 days.

NUTRIENT ANALYSIS

Calories 121 • Protein 4 g • Carbohydrate 7.2 g • Fat 8.8 g • Fiber 1.3 g • Cholesterol 0 • Sodium 4.6 mg

TOFU S'MORES

Toasting marshmallows for s'mores is a campsite ritual. Not one for sleeping in the woods, I opted for the indoor method. These easy-to-prepare treats work great with extra-firm tofu.

MAKES 12 S'MORES

COOKING NOTE
For extra-firm tofu, put the tofu, uncut, into a colander and let sit for 1 hour. This will drain out any excess water that might cause the end product to be mushy.

6 whole chocolate graham crackers

12 ounces extra-firm tofu, sliced into 12 pieces

12 teaspoons sugar or light granulated cane juice

1 cup semisweet soy chocolate chips

½ cup soy milk

1. Preheat the broiler or the oven to 500°F.

2. Cut the graham crackers in half and put a 1-ounce slice of tofu on top; place on a cookie sheet.

3. Top each slice of tofu with 1 teaspoon of sugar.

4. Broil for 3 minutes.

5. While the tofu is broiling, put the chocolate chips in a medium bowl and set aside.

6. In a small saucepan, heat the soy milk over a medium-high flame just until it starts to boil.

7. Remove from the heat and pour directly over the chocolate chips; whisk quickly until smooth.

8. Immediately, slowly and evenly pour over each tofu slice. Let cool and serve.

These cookies should be eaten fresh!

NUTRIENT ANALYSIS

Calories 140 • Protein 4.2 g • Carbohydrate 19 g • Fat 6 g • Fiber 1.1 g • Cholesterol 0 • Sodium 28 mg

SOYNUT CHOCOLATE CHIP BISCOTTI

These crispy chocolate rusks are the perfect choice to serve with coffee or after-dinner drinks. The soynuts provide extra crunch to an already hearty consistency.

MAKES 16
BISCOTTI

¾ cup whole wheat pastry flour

½ cup soy flour

½ cup sugar or light granulated cane juice

1 teaspoon baking powder

1 whole egg

⅓ cup soybean oil

½ cup soy milk

1 teaspoon vanilla extract

¼ cup soynuts, chopped

¼ cup espresso soy chocolate chips

Cinnamon sugar (optional)

1. Preheat the oven to 350°F. Line a cookie sheet with parchment paper and set aside.

2. In a mixing bowl, combine the whole wheat pastry flour, soy flour, sugar, and baking powder.

3. In an electric mixer, beat the egg with the soybean oil. Add the soy milk and vanilla.

4. Add the flour mixture to the egg mixture and mix thoroughly. Fold in the soynuts and chocolate chips.

5. Turn the dough onto a floured surface, form into two flat loaves, and place on the cookie sheet.

6. Bake for 20 minutes, remove the dough, and cut into 8 slices per loaf. Bake for another 10 minutes.

7. Sprinkle with cinnamon sugar, if desired.

These biscotti will keep in an airtight container at room temperature for 1 week.

NUTRIENT ANALYSIS

Calories 111 • Protein 3 g • Carbohydrate 13 g • Fat 5.7 g • Fiber 1.2 g • Cholesterol 0 • Sodium 28 mg

LEMON SOY BISCOTTI

Lightly scented with lemon, these soy biscotti are the perfect match for Lemon Ginger Soy Ice Cream (page 149) or just a bowl of fresh fruit. This recipe works just as well with oranges, or mix them with lemon for a strong, citrus flavor.

MAKES 16 BISCOTTI

FREEZING COOKIES

Cookie dough made with soy is easy to double and the cookies freeze beautifully. A time-saving tip is to make a double batch and wrap the extra dough tightly in plastic wrap. Store in the freezer for up to 3 months. That way, you'll be able to whip up homemade cookies at a moment's notice.

Alternatively, make a double batch of cookies and freeze the extras in airtight containers. All the cookies and biscotti will keep perfectly in the freezer for up to 3 months.

1 cup whole wheat pastry flour

¾ cup soy flour

½ cup sugar or light granulated cane juice

1 teaspoon baking powder

1 whole egg

⅓ cup soybean oil

½ cup soy milk

1 teaspoon lemon extract

Zest of 1 large lemon

1. Preheat the oven to 350°F. Line a cookie sheet with parchment paper and set aside.

2. In a mixing bowl, combine the whole wheat pastry flour, soy flour, sugar, and baking powder.

3. In an electric mixer, beat the egg with the soybean oil and add the soy milk and lemon extract.

4. Add the flour mixture to the egg mixture and mix thoroughly. Fold in the lemon zest.

5. Turn the dough onto a floured surface, form into two flat loaves, and place on the cookie sheet.

6. Bake for 25 minutes, remove the dough, and cut into 8 slices per loaf. Bake for another 10 minutes.

These biscotti will keep in an airtight container at room temperature for 1 week.

NUTRIENT ANALYSIS

Calories 110 • Protein 3.3 g • Carbohydrate 13 g • Fat 4.8 g • Fiber 1.5 g • Cholesterol 0 • Sodium 25 mg

PARFAITS, CUSTARDS, MOUSSES, PUDDINGS, AND SOY ICE CREAMS

Due to my health and fitness fanaticism, I stopped eating custard, mousse, and ice cream years ago. The traditional versions of these desserts are not necessarily bad for you, but an overindulgence can lead to many of the health risks that can be reversed just through some modification in diet. Admittedly, as a trained nutritionist, I took it to the extreme. For the periodic treat and special occasion, I turned to artificial frozen yogurt and fat-free ice creams, which were never quite as satisfying. As a result, I always felt deprived. Since I discovered soy products as alternatives to traditional ingredients, the desserts in this chapter—from the luscious Soy Milk Cappuccino Parfait to the yummy Soy Cream Tiramisù to the rich Tofu Chocolate Almond Mousse—truly combine good health with refined taste. There are now so many soy dessert products and ingredients available, it is a lot easier to follow a more healthful approach to making dessert.

These desserts taste as if they contained eggs, butter, and real dairy products—yet they incorporate soy milk, tofu, soy cream cheese, and soy yogurt, providing all the benefits of soy. You won't believe that Tofu Banana Almond Trifle could be so incredibly delicious—and yet provide 10 grams of protein and absolutely no cholesterol. And for the lactose-intolerant, the luscious richness of Chocolate Mint Soy Ice Cream with Soy Chocolate Sauce can give a whole new lease on enjoying a meal.

In contrast to traditional mousses and puddings, which require slowly cooked eggs and careful mixing to achieve the proper consistency, pureed tofu allows you to whip up luscious, creamy desserts with no effort at all. The recipes in this chapter are very simple to put together. Soy milk, tofu, and soy yogurt add richness and moistness, while soy chocolate chips melt just like regular chocolate chips. And they're just as hard to stop nibbling once you open the bag. Try them all and see: Not only am I enjoying these desserts again, I make them on a regular basis for family and friends, and continue to receive lots of compliments.

APPLE TOFU PARFAIT

This delicate parfait delivers so much pleasure for so little effort. The fluffy cream, layered between the slight firmness of the sautéed apples, gives an appealing contrast of taste and texture in one bite. Top with soynut granola for some extra crunch. When the season changes, substitute firm, ripe peaches for the apples.

1 tablespoon soybean oil

4 small Granny Smith apples, peeled and sliced thinly

1/2 cup brown sugar or dark granulated cane juice

1/3 cup apple juice

1/4-inch piece fresh ginger or 1/2 teaspoon powdered ginger

1 pound soft tofu

1/4 cup soy cream cheese

1/3 cup sugar or light granulated cane juice

1 teaspoon Calvados (apple brandy)

6 tablespoons Soynut Granola Topping (page 69)

1. Heat the soybean oil in a saucepan over medium heat; add the apples, brown sugar, apple juice, and ginger. Simmer for 10 minutes, or until the liquid is absorbed; do not dry it out completely. Set aside.

2. In a food processor or blender, combine the tofu, soy cream cheese, sugar, and Calvados and puree until smooth.

3. In a parfait glass, starting with the tofu mixture, alternate 2 tablespoons of the tofu mixture and the apple mixture twice, finishing with the tofu mixture. Repeat in each parfait glass.

4. Refrigerate for at least 2 hours. Before serving, top with soynut granola.

VARIATION

Instead of the apple mixture, alternate 3 cups of fresh berries in season with the tofu mixture.

NUTRIENT ANALYSIS

Calories 240 • Protein 6.7 g • Carbohydrate 37 g • Fat 7.9 g • Fiber 2.8 g • Cholesterol 0 • Sodium 54 mg

SOY MILK CAPPUCCINO PARFAIT

When poured into a parfait glass, this light, coffee-flavored pudding becomes an easy, elegant finish to a romantic dinner or a small dinner party.

MAKES 6 PARFAITS

2 cups soy milk

½ cup espresso or strong coffee

½ cup sugar or light granulated cane juice

3 tablespoons cornstarch

6 tablespoons soynuts

1. In a medium saucepan, heat the soy milk to a simmer.

2. In a separate bowl, combine the espresso, sugar, and cornstarch; whisk vigorously until thoroughly combined.

3. Slowly whisk the coffee mixture into the simmering soy milk. Continue to whisk until the liquid thickens, remove from the heat, and cool.

4. In a parfait glass, starting with 2 tablespoons of the soy milk mixture, alternate layers of soynuts and soy milk three times. Repeat in each parfait glass. Refrigerate for at least 2 hours before serving.

NUTRIENT ANALYSIS

Calories 96 • Protein 3.3 g • Carbohydrate 16 g • Fat 1.9 g • Fiber 1.2 g • Cholesterol 0 • Sodium 9 mg

TOFU BANANA ALMOND TRIFLE

Trifle is a regal dessert that originated in England. Fruits, nuts, and tofu cream give this version its rich look and taste. When assembling, layer the ingredients somewhat unevenly and leave overnight in the refrigerator. Serve in a decorative glass bowl for a dazzling visual effect.

**MAKES 12
SERVINGS**

1½ pounds soft tofu

¾ cup sugar or light granulated cane juice

1 tablespoon almond extract

½ cup soy cream cheese

½ cup soy milk

1 whole Soy Angel Food
Cake (page 60), cut into
1-inch cubes

3 large ripe bananas, sliced

¼ cup slivered almonds, for
garnish

2 tablespoons unsweetened
cocoa powder

1. In a food processor, combine the tofu, sugar, and almond extract; process until creamy.

2. Gradually add the soy cream cheese and soy milk, pulsing after each addition until the mixture is smooth. Process for 15 seconds.

3. In a glass bowl, layer as follows: ⅓ angel food cake cubes, ⅓ sliced bananas, ⅓ tofu mixture. Repeat and top with the slivered almonds. Refrigerate for 3 hours before serving. Dust with cocoa powder before serving.

VARIATION
Follow this procedure using individual dessert bowls.

NUTRIENT ANALYSIS
Calories 268 • Protein 10 • Carbohydrate 42 g • Fat 6.5 g • Fiber 2.3 g • Cholesterol 0 • Sodium 171 mg

TOFU BERRY TRIFLE

This is the summertime trifle that I serve to cool off my family on a hot evening. Use as many different berries as you can find to enhance the color and flavors of this refreshing treat.

**MAKES 12
SERVINGS**

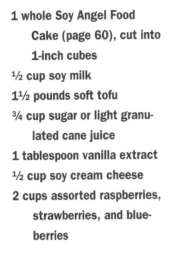

COOKING NOTE

For a winter version, use 2 cups frozen berries or sliced apples, pears, or bananas!

1 whole Soy Angel Food
    Cake (page 60), cut into
    1-inch cubes
½ cup soy milk
1½ pounds soft tofu
¾ cup sugar or light granu-
    lated cane juice
1 tablespoon vanilla extract
½ cup soy cream cheese
2 cups assorted raspberries,
    strawberries, and blue-
    berries

1. Toss the cake cubes in the soy milk, just to moisten.

2. In a food processor, combine the tofu, sugar, and vanilla; process until creamy.

3. Gradually add the soy cream cheese, pulsing after each addition until smooth.

4. Layer as follows in a trifle dish or glass bowl: arrange ⅓ cubed cake on the bottom, cover with ⅓ tofu mixture, and top with ⅓ berries. Repeat three times, finishing with berries on top. Refrigerate for 3 hours before serving.

VARIATION

Follow this procedure using individual dessert bowls.

NUTRIENT ANALYSIS

Calories 232 • Protein 9.7 g • Carbohydrate 37 g • Fat 5 g • Fiber 2.6 g • Cholesterol 0 • Sodium 171 mg

SOY CREAM TIRAMISÙ

There is a lot of folklore surrounding the origins of tiramisù, which continues to enjoy worldwide popularity. I've never met anyone who doesn't like it, and it is a great dish for entertaining. I substitute tofu and soy cream cheese for the mascarpone, and the results are outstanding.

FILLING

1 pound soft tofu

⅓ cup sugar or light granulated cane juice

½ cup soy cream cheese

1 tablespoon vanilla extract

BASE

½ cup espresso or strong brewed coffee, cool

3 tablespoons brown sugar or dark granulated cane juice

5 tablespoons unsweetened cocoa powder

24 ladyfinger cookies

1. In a food processor or blender, combine the tofu, sugar, soy cream cheese, and vanilla and puree until smooth.

2. In a separate bowl, combine the espresso, brown sugar, and 4 tablespoons of the cocoa; whisk vigorously until thoroughly combined.

3. In an 8 x 8-inch square glass pan, layer the mixtures as follows: Line the pan with 12 ladyfingers, shingled to cover the whole surface.

4. Pour half of the coffee mixture over the cookies, and then cover with half of the tofu mixture. Repeat the procedure and then cover and refrigerate for 4 hours. Right before serving sprinkle the remaining cocoa on top. Cut into 9 even squares.

This will keep, wrapped, in the refrigerator for 4 days.

NUTRIENT ANALYSIS
Calories 119 • Protein 5.3 g • Carbohydrate 11 g • Fat 5.4 g • Fiber 1 g • Cholesterol 0 • Sodium 69 mg

TOFU COCONUT CUSTARD

The coconut provides texture to this creamy and substantial eggless custard.

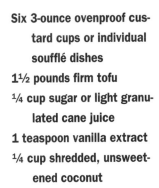

**MAKES 6
CUSTARDS**

Six 3-ounce ovenproof custard cups or individual
soufflé dishes

1½ pounds firm tofu

¼ cup sugar or light granulated cane juice

1 teaspoon vanilla extract

¼ cup shredded, unsweet-
ened coconut

1. Preheat the oven to 350°F. Lightly grease the custard cups.

2. In a food processor or blender, puree the tofu until smooth. One at a time, while blending, add the sugar and vanilla.

3. Pour the tofu mixture evenly into the custard cups and top each one with coconut.

4. Bake for 20 minutes. Cool completely and refrigerate until ready to serve.

This custard will keep, wrapped, in the refrigerator for 2 days.

NUTRIENT ANALYSIS
Calories 132 • Protein 9.2 g • Carbohydrate 11 g • Fat 6 g • Fiber 0.7 g • Cholesterol 0 • Sodium 9.8 mg

TOFU ORANGE CRÈME BRÛLÉE

My fellow chefs said it couldn't be done, but this simple tofu crème brûlée worked the first time I tried it. Feel free to use a variety of citrus fruits; they are all interchangeable here.

Six 3-ounce ovenproof custard cups or individual soufflé dishes

1½ pounds firm tofu

¼ cup sugar or light granulated cane juice

2 teaspoons orange extract

Zest of 1 orange

6 teaspoons brown sugar

1. Preheat the oven to 350°F. Lightly grease the custard cups.

2. In a food processor or blender, puree the tofu until smooth. One at a time, while blending, add the sugar, orange extract, and orange zest.

3. Pour the tofu mixture evenly into the custard cups and bake for 20 minutes.

4. Cool completely and refrigerate until ready to serve.

5. For serving, preheat the broiler. Sprinkle 1 teaspoon brown sugar on each custard and set under the broiler for 1 minute or until browned.

6. Remove from the oven and serve immediately.

NUTRIENT ANALYSIS

Calories 127 • Protein 8.9 g • Carbohydrate 13 g • Fat 3.7 g • Fiber 0.4 g • Cholesterol 0 • Sodium 9.5 mg

SOY CHOCOLATE SOUFFLÉ

This recipe is one of the few that require special attention when preparing. The delicate nature of a soufflé lends itself to a light and airy yet very satisfying dessert.

MAKES 6 SOUFFLÉS

Six 5-ounce ovenproof
    ramekins or individual
    soufflé dishes
4 tablespoons soybean oil
2 tablespoons sugar or light
    granulated cane juice
¾ cup powdered sugar
½ cup unsweetened cocoa
    powder
1 tablespoon whole wheat
    pastry flour
1 tablespoon soy flour
¼ teaspoon salt
1 cup soy milk
3 tablespoons semisweet soy
    chocolate chips
3 tablespoons Kahlúa
2 egg yolks
4 egg whites
¼ teaspoon cream of tartar
⅓ cup powdered sugar, plus
    1 tablespoon

1. Preheat the oven to 375°F. Coat the ramekins with the soybean oil and sprinkle with the sugar. Place the ramekins on a large baking pan and set aside.

2. In a mixing bowl, thoroughly combine the powdered sugar, cocoa, whole wheat pastry flour, soy flour, and salt.

3. In a saucepan, over a medium flame, heat the soy milk and stir in the flour mixture, constantly stirring with a whisk until it thickens and boils.

4. Remove from the heat, add the chocolate chips, stirring until melted. Add the Kahlúa, continue to stir, add the egg yolks, and whisk vigorously. Return to the heat and cook for 1 minute, stirring constantly.

5. Spoon the mixture into a large bowl; cool to room temperature.

6. In an electric mixer, beat together the egg whites and cream of tartar at high speed until foamy. Add ⅓ cup of the powdered sugar to the egg whites a little at a time, beating until the egg whites form stiff peaks.

7. Gently stir half of the egg white mixture into the chocolate mixture and then the remaining egg white mixture. Spoon the batter evenly into the prepared ramekins and bake for 22 minutes until puffy. Sprinkle with 1 tablespoon powdered sugar and serve immediately.

NUTRIENT ANALYSIS
Calories 174 • Protein 6.7 g • Carbohydrate 26 g • Fat 4.6 g • Fiber 2.9 g • Cholesterol 70 mg • Sodium 145 mg

TOFU CHOCOLATE ALMOND MOUSSE

Hands down, this chocolate tofu mousse can pass for the real thing. Serve it in a well-designed glass bowl as an elegant dessert, or pour it into plastic cups and give it to the kids as pudding.

MAKES 6 PORTIONS

1½ pounds regular tofu

½ cup sugar or light granulated cane juice

½ cup unsweetened cocoa powder

1 teaspoon almond extract

¼ cup almond slivers (toasting optional, see Variation), for garnish

1. In a food processor, puree the tofu until smooth. Add the sugar, cocoa, and almond extract and continue to process until thoroughly combined.

2. Pour the mixture into an airtight container and chill for 2 hours. Serve in individual dessert dishes and garnish with almond slivers.

This will keep, wrapped, in the refrigerator for 1 week.

VARIATION: TOASTING ALMONDS
Preheat the oven to 400°F. Place the almond slivers on a cookie sheet and bake for 5 to 7 minutes. Toasting brings out a strong almond flavor in the nuts.

NUTRIENT ANALYSIS
Calories 216 • Protein 13 g • Carbohydrate 22 g • Fat 8 g • Fiber 2.8 g • Cholesterol 0 • Sodium 13 mg

TOFU PUMPKIN MOUSSE

This mousse is perfect for the fall holiday season. Your guests will find it a pleasant departure from the usual pumpkin pie. Serve it family-style as part of a Thanksgiving buffet, or with Soy Gingerbread (page 90).

MAKES SIX ½-CUP PORTIONS

8 ounces soft tofu

1 cup pumpkin puree

½ cup sugar or light granulated cane juice

2 tablespoons pumpkin seeds, toasted

1. In a food processor, puree the tofu until smooth. Add the pumpkin and sugar; continue to puree until smooth.

2. Pour the mixture into an airtight container and chill for 2 hours. Serve in individual dessert dishes and garnish with pumpkin seeds.

This will keep, wrapped, in the refrigerator for 1 week.

NUTRIENT ANALYSIS

Calories 132 • Protein 5.6 g • Carbohydrate 20 g • Fat 3.6 g • Fiber 1.4 g • Cholesterol 0 • Sodium 6.2 mg

TOFU STRAWBERRY MOUSSE

The refreshing berry flavor of this Tofu Strawberry Mousse is a wonderful finish to a summer meal. The mousse also works great as a topping for cakes and quickbreads.

MAKES 6 PORTIONS

8 large strawberries, stems removed

1½ pounds regular tofu

1½ cups powdered sugar

6 whole strawberries, for garnish

1. In a food processor, puree the strawberries until they reach a thick, liquid consistency. Add the tofu and blend until fully combined.

2. Add the powdered sugar; blend until smooth.

3. Pour the mixture into an airtight container and chill for 2 hours or overnight. Serve in individual dessert dishes and garnish with whole strawberries.

This will keep, wrapped, in the refrigerator for 1 week.

NUTRIENT ANALYSIS

Calories 148 • Protein 8 g • Carbohydrate 27 g • Fat 1.4 g • Fiber 0.6 g • Cholesterol 0 • Sodium 107 mg

TOFU PINEAPPLE BREAD PUDDING

Bread pudding started out as a way for home cooks to stretch their food. Now it is as common as apple pie. The pineapple provides the perfect sweet contrast to the rich tofu cream and left-over challah. You can use any bread that you might have on hand—from white bread to croissants.

MAKES 9 PORTIONS

12 ounces soft tofu

1 cup sugar or light granulated cane juice

4 ounces soy cream cheese

¼ cup soy milk

2 teaspoons vanilla extract

4 ounces day-old challah, cubed

One 15-ounce can pineapple chunks, drained

1. Preheat the oven to 350°F. Lightly grease an 8 x 8-inch square baking pan.

2. In a food processor or blender, puree the tofu until smooth. One at a time, while blending, add the sugar, soy cream cheese, soy milk, and vanilla.

3. Place the challah cubes and pineapple chunks in the baking pan and cover with the tofu mixture.

4. Bake for 25 minutes. Cool completely and refrigerate until ready to serve.

This bread pudding will keep, wrapped, in the refrigerator for 2 days.

NUTRIENT ANALYSIS
Calories 197 • Protein 4.2 g • Carbohydrate 33 g • Fat 5.1 g • Fiber 1.3 g • Cholesterol 0 • Sodium 143 mg

CREAMY SOY MILK STICKY RICE PUDDING

This recipe is designed for a high-gluten, short-grain rice. I used the traditional kind preferred for sushi. You can also use Arborio rice, which is traditional for risotto.

MAKES 6 PORTIONS

2 cups whole vanilla soy milk

1 cup glutinous rice

2 cups whole soy milk

1 cup soy yogurt, plain or
   vanilla

½ cup sugar or light granulated cane juice

½ cup golden raisins

1 teaspoon ground cinnamon,
   for topping

1. In a large saucepan, combine the vanilla soy milk and rice and bring to a boil. Lower the heat and simmer for 10 minutes.

2. Add the whole soy milk, yogurt, sugar, and raisins.

3. Bring to a second boil and lower the heat. Simmer for 15 minutes. Stir occasionally to keep the mixture smooth.

4. Transfer the rice pudding to a glass baking pan and cool completely.

5. Refrigerate, wrapped in plastic, for 2 hours before serving. Sprinkle the cinnamon on top.

This pudding will keep, wrapped, in the refrigerator for 2 days.

NUTRIENT ANALYSIS

Calories 312 • Protein 9.5 g • Carbohydrate 58 g • Fat 4.7 g • Fiber 5.1 g • Cholesterol 0 • Sodium 40 mg

PISTACHIO SOY ICE CREAM WITH CHERRY TOPPING

This recipe is an inspiration from my childhood. Almost every Sunday night, we would go out for Chinese food, and my mother would order the pistachio cherry ice cream. I designed this dessert knowing how much she loves it, and now she can enjoy it made with soy.

MAKES 1 QUART,
OR 12 SERVINGS

1 cup pistachio nuts

2 pounds soft tofu

⅔ cup sugar or light granulated cane juice

1½ cups soy milk

1 teaspoon almond extract

1½ cups cherry pie filling

1. In a food processor, grind the pistachio nuts to a coarse consistency.

2. Add the tofu and sugar and puree.

3. While processing, add the soy milk and the almond extract and continue to process until the mixture is smooth.

4. Pour the mixture into a freezer-proof plastic container, uncovered. Stir every 15 minutes until the mixture reaches a semifrozen consistency.

5. Alternatively, pour the mixture into an electric ice cream maker and freeze according to the manufacturer's directions.

6. Serve with cherry pie filling as a topping.

COOKING NOTE
Homemade soy ice cream should be served as soon as possible. There are no additives and preservatives, so it doesn't keep as long as traditional ice cream when frozen.

NUTRIENT ANALYSIS
Calories 205 • Protein 8.5 g • Carbohydrate 24 g • Fat 8 g • Fiber 1.9 g • Cholesterol 0 • Sodium 12 mg

SOYNUT TOFU ICE CREAM

This mixture of tofu ice cream sprinkled throughout with soynuts is a natural for this cookbook. A small scoop would be perfect to serve with brownies and cookies.

MAKES 1 QUART, OR 12 SERVINGS

1½ cups soynuts

2 pounds soft tofu

⅔ cup sugar or light granulated cane juice

1½ cups soy milk

1 teaspoon almond extract

1. In a food processor, grind the soynuts to a coarse consistency.

2. Add the tofu and sugar and puree.

3. While processing, add the soy milk and the almond extract and continue to process until the mixture is smooth.

4. Pour the mixture into a freezer-proof plastic container, and place it in the freezer, uncovered. Stir every 15 minutes until the mixture reaches a semifrozen consistency.

5. Alternatively, pour the mixture into an electric ice cream maker and freeze according to the manufacturer's directions.

Serve as a topping for Soynut Pecan Pie (page 73).

NUTRIENT ANALYSIS

Calories 159 • Protein 11.8 g • Carbohydrate 15 g • Fat 5.6 g • Fiber 1.8 g • Cholesterol 0 • Sodium 12 mg

LEMON GINGER SOY ICE CREAM

The combination of soy, lemon, and ginger is decidedly Asian. Light and refreshing, this dessert has the quality of a gelato. To add a European twist, I serve it with Soy Lemon Biscotti. This ice cream also goes great with Soy Gingerbread or Soy Lemon Pound Cake.

MAKES 1 QUART, OR 12 SERVINGS

⅓ cup crystallized ginger (sugared ginger)

Zest of 3 lemons

½ teaspoon lemon extract

2 pounds soft tofu

⅔ cup sugar or light granulated cane juice

1½ cups soy milk

1. In a food processor, grind together the ginger, lemon zest, and lemon extract.

2. Add the tofu and sugar and puree.

3. While processing, add the soy milk and continue to process until the mixture is smooth.

4. Pour the mixture into a freezer-proof plastic container, and place it in the freezer, uncovered. Stir every 15 minutes until the mixture reaches a semifrozen consistency.

5. Alternatively, pour the mixture into an electric ice cream maker and freeze according to the manufacturer's directions.

NUTRIENT ANALYSIS

Calories 115 • Protein 6.8 g • Carbohydrate 15 g • Fat 3 g • Fiber 0.8 g • Cholesterol 0 • Sodium 9.8 mg

CHOCOLATE MINT SOY ICE CREAM

This rich Chocolate Mint Soy Ice Cream is a godsend for me. I cannot tolerate dairy foods due to an allergy, so I stopped eating chocolate ice cream altogether. I am back in the high life again, and living it up. I love to serve a scoop of this along with Soy Chocolate Peppermint Brownies.

MAKES 1 QUART, OR 12 SERVINGS

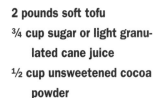

2 pounds soft tofu

¾ cup sugar or light granulated cane juice

½ cup unsweetened cocoa powder

1½ cups soy milk

1 teaspoon mint extract

1. In a food processor, puree the tofu until smooth.

2. Add the sugar and cocoa and process until well blended.

3. While processing, add the soy milk and mint extract; continue to process until the mixture is smooth.

4. Pour the mixture into a freezer-proof plastic container, and place it in the freezer, uncovered. Stir every 15 minutes until the mixture reaches a semifrozen consistency.

5. Alternatively, pour the mixture into an electric ice cream maker and freeze according to the manufacturer's directions.

NUTRIENT ANALYSIS

Calories 117 • Protein 7.5 g • Carbohydrate 14 g • Fat 3.3 g • Fiber 1.5 g • Cholesterol 0 • Sodium 10 mg

BANANA CHOCOLATE CHIP SOY ICE CREAM

The rich banana flavor, accented by the soy chocolate chips, makes this winning combination of fruit and chocolate a hit. Serve with Banana Soy Chocolate Chip Walnut Squares for a mini-feast.

MAKES 1 QUART, OR 12 SERVINGS

3 bananas, very ripe

2 pounds soft tofu

¾ cup sugar or light granulated cane juice

1½ cups soy milk

½ cup semisweet soy chocolate chips

1. In a food processor, puree the bananas.

2. Add the tofu and sugar and puree.

3. While processing, add the soy milk and continue to process until the mixture is smooth. Fold in the chocolate chips.

4. Pour the mixture into a freezer-proof plastic container, and place it in the freezer, uncovered. Stir every 15 minutes until the mixture reaches a semifrozen consistency.

5. Alternatively, pour the mixture into an electric ice cream maker and freeze according to the manufacturer's directions.

NUTRIENT ANALYSIS
Calories 159 • Protein 7.5 g • Carbohydrate 23 g • Fat 4.8 g • Fiber 1.8 g • Cholesterol 0 • Sodium 9.4 mg

COCONUT SOY ICE CREAM WITH SOY CHOCOLATE SAUCE

For additional coconut flavor, toast half of the shredded coconut and add it to the electric ice cream maker right before serving. When this ice cream is topped with Soy Chocolate Sauce, you'll never miss the cream.

MAKES 1 QUART, OR 12 SERVINGS

½ cup shredded, unsweetened coconut

1½ cups soy milk

2 pounds soft tofu

¾ cup sugar or light granulated cane juice

1½ cups Soy Chocolate Sauce (recipe follows)

1. In a glass bowl, place the coconut in the soy milk and set aside for 10 minutes.

2. In a food processor, combine the tofu and sugar; puree until smooth.

3. While processing, add the coconut and soy milk and continue to process until smooth.

4. Pour the mixture into a freezer-proof plastic container, and place it in the freezer, uncovered. Stir every 15 minutes until the mixture reaches a semifrozen consistency.

5. Alternatively, pour the mixture into an electric ice cream maker and freeze according to the manufacturer's directions. Serve with the Soy Chocolate Sauce.

NUTRIENT ANALYSIS

Calories 116 • Protein 6.9 g • Carbohydrate 13 g • Fat 4.1 g • Fiber 0.9 g • Cholesterol 0 • Sodium 9.8 mg

Soy Chocolate Sauce

**1 cup semisweet soy choco-
late chips**
1½ cups whole soy milk

In a saucepan on medium heat, melt the chocolate chips in the soy milk, whisking until smooth. Cool to room temperature and serve with all flavors of soy ice cream.

This sauce will keep in the refrigerator for 2 weeks.

NUTRIENT ANALYSIS

Calories 75 • Protein 1.3 g • Carbohydrate 9 g • Fat 4.6 g • Fiber 2 g • Cholesterol 0 • Sodium 5 mg

SOY CHEDDAR CHEESE AND APPLES WITH DIPPING SAUCE

During a multicourse meal, it is customary to serve a cheese course after the main entrée has been completed. Using soy cheese, you cut the fat in half, and the feeling of fullness with it. This cheese plate can double as a dessert or a snack, and the dipping sauce is a delightful touch.

MAKES 6 SERVINGS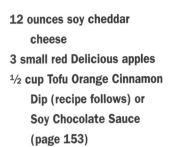

12 ounces soy cheddar cheese

3 small red Delicious apples

½ cup Tofu Orange Cinnamon Dip (recipe follows) or Soy Chocolate Sauce (page 153)

1. Slice the soy cheese into 6 slices the long way and then in half to form 12 squares.

2. Core and slice the apples, leaving the skin on for color.

3. Shingle the apple and cheese slices on a round platter and place the sauce of choice in the middle.

Serve immediately.

NUTRIENT ANALYSIS

Calories 180 • Protein 12 g • Carbohydrate 12 g • Fat 8 g • Fiber 1.8 g • Cholesterol 0 • Sodium 380 mg

---

Tofu Orange Cinnamon Dip

12 ounces soft tofu

½ cup soy milk

1 teaspoon orange extract

Zest of 1 orange

¼ teaspoon ground cinnamon

In a food processor, puree the tofu and soy milk until smooth. Continue to process and add the orange extract, orange zest, and cinnamon until fully combined. Refrigerate until ready to use.

This dip will keep up to a week.

NUTRIENT ANALYSIS

Calories 49 • Protein 5.0 g • Carbohydrate 2 g • Fat 2.2 g • Fiber 0.6 g • Cholesterol 0 • Sodium 6.6 mg

SOY SOURCE GUIDE

Products made from soy are widely available in most grocery stores, supermarkets, and health food stores worldwide. If you have difficulty locating certain products, call or write the following companies. Included are sources for kitchen equipment as well. They will be able to direct you to the nearest distributor or fill your needs by mail order.

ADAM'S ORGANIC COFFEES
415 Voelker Drive
San Mateo, CA 94403
(800) 339-2326
www.adamsorganiccoffees.com
Organic coffees from all over the world

ARCHER DANIELS MIDLAND (ADM)
P.O. Box 1470
Decatur, IL 62525
(800) 637-5850
www.admworld.com
The country's largest producer of soy products

ARROWHEAD MILLS
P.O. Box 2059
Hereford, TX 79045
(800) 749-0730
www.arrowheadmills.com
Organic flours, grains, beans, and cereals

BOB'S RED MILL
5209 SE International Way
Milwaukie, OR 97222
(503) 654-3215
www.bobsredmill.com
Organic flours and grains

CLOUD NINE, TROPICAL SOURCE ORGANIC CHOCOLATES
300 Observer Highway, 3rd floor
Hoboken, NJ 07030
(201) 216-0382
www.cloudninecandy.com
Organic chocolates, specializing in the soy-based chocolate chips

CMC BAKERY
800 Ela Road
Lake Zurich, IL 60047
(800) 238-2253
www.bakingpans.com
Commercial and domestic bakeware

CUISINART
P.O. Box 2160
Hightstown, NJ 08520
(800) 726-9499
www.cuisinart.com
A full line of kitchen equipment including food
processors and ice cream makers

DR SOY
15375 Barranca Parkway, #B101
Irvine, CA 92618
(800) 377-6920
www.drsoy.com
Soynuts, trail mix, and cereals

EDEN FOODS
701 Tecumseh Road
Clinton, MI 49236
(517) 456-7474
www.edensoy.com
Soy milk and tofu

ENER-G FOODS
P.O. Box 84487
Seattle, WA 98124-5787
(800) 331-5222
www.ener-g.com
Egg replacer powder

FLORIDA CRYSTALS
50 Coconut Row
Palm Beach, FL 35480
(800) 443-2767
www.floridacrystals.com
Organic sugars and light granulated cane juice

GALAXY FOODS
2441 Viscount Row
Orlando, FL 32809
(407) 855-5500
www.galaxyfoods.com
A great source for soy cheese, soy cream cheese,
and soy sour cream

GENISOY PRODUCTS
2300 S. Watney Way, #D
Fairfield, CA 94533
(888) 436-4769
Soynuts

HINOICHI TOFU
7351 Orangewood Avenue
Garden Grove, CA 92841
(714) 901-4350
www.house-foods.com
Organic tofu

I.M. HEALTHY SOYNUT BUTTER
4220 Commercial Way
Glenview, IL 60025
(800) 288-1012
imhsoynutbutter@aol.com

KING ARTHUR FLOUR COMPANY
P.O. Box 876
Norwich, VT 05055
(800) 827-6836
www.kingarthurflour.com
Flours and specialty bakeware

KITCHENAID
701 Main Street
Joseph, MI 49085
(800) 541-6390
www.kitchenAid.com
Electric mixers and food processors

LIZ NSPIRED NATURAL FOODS
14855 Wicks Boulevard
San Leandro, CA 94577
(510) 686-0116
www.nspiredfoods.com
Chocolate and soynut butter

MORI NU
2050 West 190th Street, #110
Torrance, CA 90504
(800) 669-8638
www.morinu.com
Specially sealed, airtight, 12.3-ounce packages of
tofu

NORDICWARE
5005 Highway 7
Minneapolis, MN 55416
(800) 328-4310
www.nordicware.com
Unusual designs and sizes of specialty bakeware

SOYAKAAS CHEESES
P.O. Box 1067
St. Augustine, FL 32085
(800) 238-3947
Organic, nonhydrogenated soy cheeses

SOY-SATION
9001 SE Lawnfield Road
Clackamas, OR 97015
(503) 652-1988
Soy and nut-based cheese products

SPECTRUM NATURALS
1304 Southpoint Boulevard, #280
Petaluma, CA 94954
(800) 995-2705
www.spectrumnaturals.com
Organic oils and nonhydrogenated margarine

SUCANAT (WHOLESOME FOODS)
P.O. Box 2860
Daytona Beach, FL 32120
(912) 651-4820
www.wholesomefoods.com
Organic, dark granulated cane juice

SUR LA TABLE
Mail Order Division
1765 Sixth Avenue South
Seattle, WA 98134
(800) 243-0852
www.surlatable.com
Specialty foods and cookware

TOFUTTI BRANDS, INC.
50 Jackson Drive
Cranford, NJ 07016
(908) 272-2400
www.tofutti.com
Soy cream cheese, sour cream, and assorted
frozen dessert products

VITASOY USA
400 Oyster Point Boulevard, #201
San Francisco, CA 94080
(800) 848-2769
www.vitasoy-usa.com
Organic soy milk and tofu

WHITE WAVE, INC.
1990 North 57th Court
Boulder, CO 80301
(303) 443-3470
www.whitewave.com
Organic tofu, soy milk, and soy yogurt

THE WHOLESOY COMPANY
49 Stevenson Street, Suite 1075
San Francisco, CA 94105
(415) 495-2870
www.wholesoycom.com
Soy milk and soy yogurt

WILDWOOD NATURAL FOODS
135 Bolinas Road
Fairfax, CA 94930
(800) 499-8638
www.wildwoodnaturalfoods.com
Organic tofu and other soy products

WILLIAMS-SONOMA
P.O. Box 7456
San Francisco, CA 94120
(800) 541-2233
www.williams-sonoma.com
Specialty cookware

WILTON INDUSTRIES
2240 West 75th Street
Woodbridge, IL 60517
(800) 772-7111
www.wilton.com
Baking and cake decorating supplies

For general information about soy—its medical and health benefits and how to use it—write or e-mail the author:

PATRICIA GREENBERG
"The Joy of Soy"
P.O. Box 10853
Beverly Hills, CA 90213
www.joyofsoy.com

For soyfood industry information, write or e-mail:

THE SOYFOODS ASSOCIATION OF NORTH AMERICA
1723 U Street N.W.
Washington, DC 20009
(202) 986-5600
www.soyfoods.org

U.S. SOYFOODS DIRECTORY
Steven's & Associates
4816 North Pennsylvania Street
Indianapolis, IN 46205-1744
1 800 talk soy
info@soyfoods.com
This directory is published annually.

INDEX

pumpkin, 23
  soy nut loaf, 92
  tofu mousse, 143
  tofu pie, 72

quickbreads, 83–96
  banana soy chocolate chip wal-
    nut squares, 93
  chocolate soy hearts with cashew
    soy cream frosting, 95–96
  soy carrot rectangles with cream
    cheese frosting, 88–89
  soy chocolate chip coffee ring, 87
  soy gingerbread, 90
  soy lemon pound cake, 91
  soy orange spice squares, 94
  soy pumpkin nut loaf, 92

raisin(s), 22
  in Italian "tofu ricotta" tart, 82
  oatmeal soynut cookies, 123
raspberries, in tofu berry trifle, 136
raspberry jam:
  sauce, marble tofu cheesecake
    with, 57–58
  soy chocolate brownies, 105–6
  in soy yellow layer cake with soy
    chocolate cream cheese frost-
    ing, 41–42
rice, 22
  pudding, creamy soy milk sticky,
    146

salt, 23–24
sauces, 6
  raspberry, raspberry marble tofu
    cheesecake with, 57–58
  soy chocolate, coconut soy ice
    cream with, 152–53
  soy chocolate, soy cheddar
    cheese and apples with, 154
  tofu orange cinnamon dip, soy
    cheddar cheese and apples
    with, 154–55
scones:
  apricot soy, 109
  orange soy chocolate chip, 110
seeds, 21, 22

sodium, 11–12, 17
soufflé, soy chocolate, 140–41
sour cream, soy, 6, 15, 83
soy, 4, 5–7
  almond drop cookies, 125
  angel food cake, 60
  apricot scones, 109
  banana chocolate chip ice cream,
    151
  banana chocolate chip walnut
    squares, 93
  banana cream pie, tropical, with
    pineapple and macadamia
    nuts, 77
  banana cupcakes, with soy cream
    cheese walnut frosting,
    99–100
  blood orange cake, with soy
    cream cheese frosting, 47–48
  carrot ginger pie, 71
  carrot rectangles, with soy cream
    cheese frosting, 88–89
  cheddar cheese and apples, with
    dipping sauce, 154–55
  chocolate angel food cakes, mini,
    61
  chocolate chip coffee ring, 87
  chocolate cream pie, 75–76
  chocolate devil's food cupcakes,
    with chocolate soy milk
    frosting, 97–98
  chocolate hazelnut cake, with soy
    chocolate ganache, 38–39
  chocolate hearts, with cashew
    soy cream frosting, 95–96
  chocolate layer cake, with choco-
    late soynut butter frosting,
    51–52
  chocolate maple cake, with
    chocolate almond soy frost-
    ing, 49–50
  chocolate mint ice cream, 150
  chocolate peppermint brownies,
    107
  chocolate raspberry brownies,
    105–6
  chocolate soufflé, 140–41
  chocolate truffles, assorted, 117

  coconut ice cream, with soy
    chocolate sauce, 152–53
  cream pie topping, 76
  cream tiramisù, 137
  fudgy chocolate bundt cake,
    with tofu chocolate mocha
    and vanilla drizzles,
    35–37
  gingerbread, 90
  lemon biscotti, 128
  lemon ginger ice cream, 149
  lemon pound cake, 91
  mango poppyseed cake, 44
  maple cupcakes, with maple
    syrup frosting, 103–4
  miniature peach upside-down
    cakes, 59
  orange chocolate chip scones,
    110
  orange spice squares, 94
  pistachio ice cream, with cherry
    topping, 147
  pomegranate cake, with soy
    chocolate ganache, 40
  products, 12–18
  pumpkin nut loaf, 92
  strawberry layer cake, with tofu
    coconut cream frosting,
    45–46
  tollhouse cookies, 122
  yellow layer cake, with soy
    chocolate cream cheese frost-
    ing, 41–42
  see also butter, soynut; cheese,
    soy; chocolate chips, soy;
    cream cheese, soy; cream
    cheese frosting, soy; milk,
    soy; soynuts; tofu; yogurt,
    soy
soy angel food cake, 60
  chocolate, mini, 61
  in tofu banana almond trifle,
    135
  in tofu berry trifle, 136
soybean oil, 18, 50
soybeans, 3, 12–13
  characteristics of, 5–6
  history of, 3–4